# splankna

Here, let me help...

[**spläwnk** • nuh]

*The Redemption of Energy Healing
for the Kingdom of God*

## sarah j. thiessen

CrossHouse Publishing
2844 S. FM 549
Suite A
Rockwall, TX 75032
www.crosshousebooks.com

ISBN: 978-1-61315-013-9
Library of Congress: 2011936349

# Acknowledgements

Thank you, Heather, for being my Jonathan.

Thank you, Linda, for your relentless hopefulness and ease.

Thank you, Pixie, for your faithfulness and gentleness.

Thank you, George, for being such an advocate
and bringing some testosterone to the Institute.

Thank you, Gail, for forcing me to carve out the time
to make this happen.

Thank you, Rick, for ripping this book to shreds. It was
indispensable.

Thank you, Brian, for being so naturally redemptive.
You make a sharp tool.

Thank you Profs—Eddie, Waymon, and Tom.
You'll never know your full impact.

Thank you, Alex, for being the first person whose life
God changed through Splankna.

Thank you, my wonderful man. God gave you to me to keep my
feet on the ground and my heart at peace.

# Contents

A Note to the Reader................................................................7

Introduction .........................................................................9

Chapter 1: Getting Here ..........................................................15

Chapter 2: The Basics of Energy................................................33

Chapter 3: Energy in Psychology .............................................43

Chapter 4: The Basics of New Age..............................................65

Chapter 5: Our Response to New Age .......................................83

Chapter 6: Energy in the Bible.................................................97

Chapter 7: The Redemptive Posture.........................................107

Chapter 8: The Basics of Witchcraft .......................................121

Chapter 9: Redemption in Witchcraft? (Surely not!) .............131

Chapter 10: What is Splankna Therapy? ................................149

Chapter 11: The Redemptive Thinker ....................................161

Chapter 12: The Impassioned Plea.........................................175

Appendix............................................................................181

References ..........................................................................183

Index.................................................................................189

About Splankna ..................................................................193

# A Note to the Reader

To the Skeptic:

Hats off to you. I'm married to one, and I love him dearly. I have only one request. Please read the whole book.

To the Liberal:

Please take the boundaries seriously. All things are permissible, but not all things are beneficial.

*Holy Spirit, we invite you to teach, correct, and inspire.*

# Introduction

*"When my son, Brandon, was 3-years old, he sustained a head injury in an accident. Physically, he healed quickly. However, emotionally, he was in real trouble. My bold and brave boy was experiencing panic attacks, as well as obsessive and irrational behaviors. He lived in fear and did not feel safe under anyone's care, except mine. Doctors told me that the concussion altered his personality. The only remedy was to medicate my son. My husband and I refused to mask his symptoms by drugging him. We still praise God for leading us to Splankna Therapy! We were able to gently free my son from the fear, mistrust, and panic that controlled his life. His healing still brings tears to my eyes. I have my boy back! He is once again taking on the world around him, bold and brave!"* —Brandon's Mom

*"Splankna Therapy truly rescued me—so much so that it's kind of hard to put into words. I feel like it saved my life. God used this therapy to reveal things about my story and heal me in places that were so shut down and damaged in my body and soul. We're talking REAL healing here! Places that I highly doubt I could have been brought to through talking alone. I am so deeply thankful. I've recommended many, many friends of many different circles and philosophies. All have come away with noticeable*

9

*change. It's so exciting to finally see this beautiful gift of God becoming available for more people!" —Steve M.*

*"I began this work because of a dark cloud that colored my days and nights after the death of my wife. The cloud has lightened and been truly lifted. Our work together has alleviated fears stemming from a very traumatic year, my fifth, spent 24/7 at a nursery while my mother was quarantined with tuberculosis. Mind-body work has been very effective at leading me on toward the healing that God has for me. With gratitude . . ." —LOH*

*"I started this work because I realized I was only dating alcoholics. I didn't want to end up marrying one. I wanted a healthy relationship with a partner. Over the years, I noticed patterns in who I was attracted to. It was becoming more clear; I was scared for my life and my future. I also had a paralyzing fear of flying which was really a problem for me since I love to travel internationally. That fear is gone completely! I used to get panic attacks, sweaty palms, and a racing heart rate. Now all I have is peace and quiet during flights! Through the work we have done on the relationship side, I have noticed real, tangible changes in myself. I feel valuable. I can walk into a supermarket and give a smile to strangers instead of lowering my head as I pass by. My eye contact is better in general. My relationships at work have improved. I find myself less defensive; that makes work a better place. The changes aren't something we made by saying OK, let's improve your eye contact. Those are side benefits to feeling forgiven/forgiveness, self-love, and self-worth. I have a long way to go. I know that. But I am a better Me today than I was before I started this. God has used it to change my life." —Laurie L.*

*"I am a physician and stopped practicing contemporary medicine because I had seen countless patients succumb to various psychoemotional/ spiritual issues that were beyond their conscious*

*control, thus derailing their healing process. I was in search of a program that would enable me to unleash everyone's true potential to walk with God. Well, that modality is Splankna Therapy, which I might add has helped me to be a better practitioner, father, husband, and fellow human being. I have been in search of healing since 1988 and have done just about every kind of therapy you can imagine and then some. Splankna has allowed me to feel God's presence on a much larger scale without succumbing to the constant booby traps that the enemy lays down for us all. Splankna is the most powerful therapy I know of to realize Christ's gift and serve our fellow man." —Dr. H. Johnson*

These are a few testimonies from Splankna Therapy clients over the years. They experienced God working in their lives in wonderful ways. Splankna is a Christian protocol for Energy Psychology. As far as I am aware, it represents the first formal attempt within the Christian psychological community to formulate a protocol for Energy Psychology from a biblical foundation. This book addresses some challenging questions that arise on the topic.

How should a Christian respond to the world of energy healing? The development of quantum physics has introduced a unique set of apologetic challenges to the Body of Christ. The fields of Energy Medicine and Energy Psychology require us to ask new questions and explore uncharted ground. Our society is running full speed ahead into the world of quantum energy and its myriad of possible applications. What is the position of the Church, of Scripture? This is a call to the Christian community to redeem the world of quantum energy and its applications for the Kingdom of God and a blueprint for how to go about it.

The field of Energy Psychology will be our point of reference, although the discussion is meant to apply to Energy Medicine as well, and other topics relevant to redemption. We will discuss the major arguments against the Christian's use of Energy Psychology— namely that it is New Age and witchcraft. We will explore Scripture's voice in the matter as well.

Throughout human history, fundamental alterations in thought are resisted. We are naturally afraid of change. When Louis Pasteur discovered in 1860 that we are constantly surrounded by tiny, invisible microbes called germs, the French Press responded,

> "I am afraid that the experiments you quote, M. Pasteur, will turn against you. The world into which you wish to take us is really too fantastic."

It's instinctive to resist a significant shift in worldview. I encourage you to keep that in mind while you read. Notice any subtle fears that arise through the process. Before you read this, ask the Holy Spirit to place a sieve over your mind and heart so that only what the Lord intends can take root—nothing more, but nothing less either. In all things, Lordship is the issue. Wading through the topics of New Age, quantum physics, and witchcraft will highlight that truth.

The questions presented in this book are important. As the Body of Christ we need to address them. But ultimately, the point of this book is not to get the Christian community comfortable with acupuncture, energy healing, Splankna Therapy, or any other practice in particular. The point is to advance the Kingdom of God; healing is one of the fundamental signs of its presence. The point is to equip Christians to move from the defense to the offense in our culture. To become so clear about the truth and the lies surrounding us that we can move compellingly into our society and not just keep ourselves safe from it. We will use Splankna Therapy as an example, but its defense is not the main issue. Primarily this is meant to be an exercise in learning to think redemptively when it comes to the current healing culture. There are boundaries we have muddied; there is life we have forfeited.

My hope for you as the reader is twofold: that you understand how Splankna Therapy is an example of a useful and truly Christian healing protocol and that you come away with a clear structure for evaluating any healing protocol through a biblical lens. My hope is that you find this book both wildly liberal and fiercely conservative at the same time.

May you find a new freedom in practice,

A deeper challenge in holiness,

And new armor to represent Him well,

For such a time as this.

But first some of the story. I was never going to be this person.

# CHAPTER 1

# Getting Here

*"I do not feel obliged to believe that the same God
who had endowed us with sense, reason and intellect
has intended us to forgo their use." —Galileo*

In Southern California the Church of Christ is a little more liberal than it is in other parts of the country. It is a conservative denomination best known for *a capella* singing and baptism as the point of salvation. In this vein of Christianity a strong emphasis is placed on biblical knowledge, personal holiness, and evangelism. A wonderful family feeling exists in the Churches of Christ. But unfortunately very little emphasis is placed on the Holy Spirit, dealing with the enemy, or any forms of power for the believer. This is not the sort of beginning one would expect for the author of a book like this one. But strengths and weaknesses combined, it was a beginning I wouldn't trade. It gave me a start in the Word that has proved indispensable.

Both of my parents came from a long heritage of believers (and belonging to the Church of Christ) as far back as we can trace. The things I have done with my life would usually bring about a fair amount of warfare, but these many generations of faithfulness to God have allowed me measures of freedom for which I am so grateful. I have no conscious memory of ever *not* knowing God. I was born on a pew. I have no recollection of ever being without the strong heart's knowing that God and I were intimately connected and that I belonged to Him. I used to feel awkward when people would ask for my testimony about coming to Christ because I don't have one. My very earliest memories are washed in a worldview of faith. I was the kid who won the Bible Bowl every summer at Christian camp and knew all the words to "When I Survey" by the time I was 3-years old (and its four-part harmony of course, due to all that *a capella* singing).

In my family, church was the whole world; I thought it was that way for everyone. My father was a deacon for a while and led singing as often as he could. My mother had a stint as church secretary when we were young and taught innumerable little horseshoe-shaped, bright-eyed Sunday school groups. All of my friends were at church. Every boy I ever dated was from youth group or Christian college. I was one of those people who could fairly be accused of growing up in a Christian bubble and being out of touch with the real world. But there are worse accusations. I did go to public school in Los Angeles. I was a minority there in a pretty rough school where kids were bussed in from other parts of the city. I went through junior high and high school afraid much of the time, so at least I earned a few world-savvy points.

During those years I thought we were the perfect family. It is a remarkable grace of God that He wires children that way—to innocently assume the best of parents. Have you ever noticed that all children think their mother is beautiful, their father is a superhero, and their family is rich? It's great. God gives parents a beautiful handicap. My parents were loving toward us and were devoted believers, but they were very unhappily married. They did their best to honor God and hang in there, but it was painful for everyone. They finally divorced when I was 12-years old.

I bring the divorce up because it was also the first soil that grew my relationship with God. Divorce is like an earthquake. The fact that the ground beneath us doesn't move and we can count on that allows us to tolerate the fact that everything else does move. It's a stable platform to handle the instability. Happily married parents are the same way. Knowing that your parents' love will always be an institution provides basic stability. It's fundamental. It allows you to tolerate all the outside messes of life. But when your parents are not OK, it's like the very ground beneath your feet can't be trusted. They split up; the earth quakes.

In the midst of that earthquake I turned to God. I remember being very young, lying in bed at night, listening to them fight when they thought we were asleep and thinking to myself, "No matter what happens—even if they divorce, even if *the mountains fall into the heart of the sea* (Ps. 46:2), I'm OK, because my forever is OK with God." Looking back it feels like I was forced by the pain and volatility of their conflict to really rely on God. I was practicing the injunction to cast my cares on Him and let His peace guard my heart and mind. He did give me His peace and taught me how to rest in it. I'm grateful for that. He is faithful to work all things for good for those who believe.

That season also forced me into some of the deeper questions about life with God. Holiness seemed fairly self-explanatory, but what about faith? What did it mean to live faithfully on a Tuesday morning? What about decisions? How could one navigate life without knowing the perfect will of God? Why does such a discrepancy exist between the reality painted in the New Testament and what we experience in daily life? How is it that God is "good" in the face of the pain and tragedy that He allows? These sorts of questions and many others were very tangible to me even before my teen years. It was always my nature to wrestle.

## Diving into Psych

Armed with all of my questions and a deep attachment to God, it came time for college. I was sure that I wanted to go to a Christian school. I went to Abilene Christian University in Texas. But I had no idea what I wanted to be when I grew up, so I worked through the first two years of core courses and tried out a few possible majors. I had always been a singer and was even dabbling in guitar during my freshman year (ah, the cliché), so I tried a course in the music department. It took me about three days to discover I was not a student of music, just an enjoyer. My only other interests were faith and psychology. As a female in the Church of Christ there is little point in getting a Bible degree, since women do not do professional ministry. My other main interest was psychology, but my only impression of that field was from a worldly perspective. I didn't want to devote myself to a study and practice so apparently godless and futile. So I floated around aimlessly for a while until one day when someone told me about the Marriage and Family Therapy Institute at ACU—a graduate degree in psychology from a biblical foundation. I was instantly sold.

Since there were no specific undergraduate degree requirements for acceptance into the graduate program, I decided I was free to be a Bible major, female or not. I was one of only two women in the whole theology department at that time. I had a wonderful time. I felt like a fly on the wall of man-world, getting a glimpse into their fraternity secrets. The Church of Christ is very devoted to male leadership. It really was a bit of a coup to be there in the traditionally male-dominated degree program. One of our core courses was Homiletics (preaching class). At the end of the semester when we each had to give a sermon to the class and professor, I came to class in a three-piece suit and tie, just for fun. Overall I had a great time during those few years. It felt too good to be true to study and write about Scripture and get a degree for it. And then, with a Bachelor's in Youth and Family Ministry under my belt, the time came for graduate school.

My graduate degree consisted of traditional therapeutic training with an emphasis on "systems theory"—the viewing of families as "systems" that follow similar rules that apply to all systems: in science, nature, and sociology. Systems theory teaches that psychological symptoms have some useful function within their original context. Clients are not seen as individually "crazy". Rather, it is assumed that the symptoms they're presenting began as functional ways to deal with some earlier context— typically the childhood family system. As it turned out, this "functional" orientation around symptoms would serve me well in the surprising path that God had in mind.

I thoroughly enjoyed graduate school as well, although I was continually frustrated with the lack of measurable change I saw in clients, no matter what tactic was taken. I chalked it up to inexperience and assumed results would improve as I developed as a therapist (and I'm sure they would have had I continued in that path). I completed my grad-school internship with a clear goal in mind. I wanted to be a part of one of the national Christian group practices like Minirth-Meier or Samaritan Counseling Centers. Our little graduating class of fledgling therapists consisted of 21 cohorts. In the few months before graduation everyone started accepting his or her various first counseling positions, but nothing was happening for me. I interviewed for a job in in-patient psych in North Carolina, but it felt overwhelming. I was unprepared for that kind of intensity. Nothing else was panning out. My roommate at the time had her own clear goal in mind. She didn't care what the job was as long as she could live in Colorado. She just had to have one of those license plates with the green mountains on it.

She interviewed with several different positions along the Front Range and ended up, by means I can't recall, taking a position in a very small town in the Midwest, where it turned out her entire birth family was still living. She was adopted and had been looking for them for a while. It was a really remarkable move of God in her life. The day after she accepted the job in Illinois, the Samaritan Counseling Center in south Denver called to offer her a position. While on the phone with them she literally said "Well, I've taken another job, but my roommate's right here . . . she has the same credentials." She handed me the phone. That became my oh-so-prestigious entrance into the field.

## Brutal Redirection

I trekked out to Denver to interview for that position with the Samaritan Counseling Center. I was supposed to give a case study in their weekly group therapists' meeting. I was in graduate school mode and accustomed to giving case studies of problem clients—ones where you were stuck and needed input. Unbeknownst to me, they expected me to give a *success* case study and were thoroughly impressed with my vulnerability and confidence in exposing a personal therapy debacle in an interview. "Oh . . . yes, I meant to do that." I accepted the position with them gladly and thought I was off to a great start—right in line with my expected path.

I packed up my meager college student belongings, hooked up my little Honda to the back of a U-Haul semi, and headed for Denver. Another fellow graduate student was a native there. His parents had agreed for me to stay in their basement for a few weeks while I found an apartment. Little did I know that a few weeks would turn into seven months. I arrived at Samaritan for my first day on the job, self-conscious and excited, only to be told "Oh, we're sorry, but we don't have that job anymore." Samaritan operates by opening satellite offices in churches. The churches involved have a financial obligation in the deal. The church I was hired to work with had backed out for that reason. So there I was. I had moved, all alone, to an unfamiliar city for my dream job that no longer existed. For seven months I stayed on with them without pay and tried to help them secure another satellite office arrangement so that I could have a job, but nothing ever came together. I worked several executive-assistant-type temp jobs until I finally succumbed to the inevitable.

When I was in graduate school, I always said I would do anything in the field of psychology except residential adolescent work. I didn't do well with teenagers back then. I tended to get triggered by entitlement. And of course, when I had spent seven months trying to find another job, the only positions available in Colorado were . . . "Adolescent day treatment with a residential component" . . . lovely. Now by this point I had walked with God since childhood. I knew that He could be sneaky. I reasoned, "God probably knows that I will love this kind of work. He had to force me into it to find that out. It will probably be the best thing I've ever done."

Well, it wasn't. It was actually a little worse than I had anticipated. The upsides were that I had a fabulous director who was supportive, terrific with the kids, and really helped me grow in self-awareness both in strengths and weaknesses of mine, and that I was able to get my practicum hours completed so I could sit for my licensure exams. But the rest was downside. I spent 14 months working there at Halcyon with "the 10-percent toughest kids in the state". I did my best to reach the kids, but it felt impossible most of the time. I was too young and inexperienced to know what they needed or whether I had it to give. The combination of the entitlement, which I was already so triggered by, and the social services system that often does more harm than good left me feeling debilitated and hopeless.

It was also really difficult to be a believer in that environment. I had my personal computer in my office with a little sticker across the top that had been there all through graduate school to help me keep my head on straight through all the "sitting-at-the-feet-of-the-masters" kind of schooling. It read simply, "God is my teacher." They made me remove it from my private computer in my private office because we were in a government facility. I was doing family co-therapy for about six months with a much more experienced male therapist who was an atheist. We worked together very well until one week our client family came bounding into the office, excited to tell us that the previous Sunday they had all accepted Christ and been baptized. Because I celebrated with them, my co-therapist tried to get me fired for poor boundaries and undermining his rapport with them.

One depressive summer afternoon, there at Boulder County Mental Health, fresh from another therapeutic hold with a spitting, cussing, biting 12-year-old and feeling particularly desperate, I cold-called Minirth-Meier in the Denver Tech Center. Cold call turned warm as I happened to get the director on the phone. They hired me to, once again, open a satellite office—this time in Limon, CO. I and another therapist made plans with them through the rest of the summer to start this new venture. I felt like I was back on track. This was the kind of career I had had in mind all along. I trained the next therapist to take my place in the treatment milieu at Halcyon and with the key to the Limon office in hand had the big goodbye dinner with the kids.

I got home that night to my Westminster apartment and was greeted by a voicemail that said something like this: "We're really sorry, but we're taking on several therapists at the same time and realized we can't guarantee all of you enough referrals. We really like you, but we had to cut someone; you're the only one without previous private practice experience. We're going to have to back out of the deal." I was stunned. This was the second time this sort of thing had happened to me. I was not even licensed yet. God did not seem to agree with my plan.

Needless to say I was starting to get bitter with Him by this point. As far as I could see, I had followed His laws. I had taken the high road, delayed gratification, gone straight through two college degrees trying to honor Him in my life choices, and He was cutting me off at the knees at every turn. I had also managed to get through six years of Christian college and remain single. Alone that night, staring down from the third floor window, I felt like God was betraying me on every front.

I failed to mention that when Samaritan landed the bombshell on me a year and half earlier, I woke up the next morning to open doors everywhere. But they were pointing in the wrong direction. They were all about going into private practice. The morning after finding out I had moved to Denver for a job that no longer existed, I got offers for office space of my own, advertising, referral sources, the works. But I was fresh out of graduate school. How presumptuous would it be to go into private practice as a Marriage and Family Therapist when I was only 24-years old, didn't have a license, and didn't even have a marriage or family. This couldn't possibly be God's leading. I dismissed those open doors as unreasonable and signed up with the local temp agency.

Well, when everything was cut out from under me for the second time with Minirth-Meier, He did the same thing. The next morning, jobless and angry, I woke to find a leasing company handing me office space, advertising breaks, referral sources, and everything. This was too familiar. God was up to something. So this time, partially in spite, I must admit, I took the leap. I said to God, "Well, since this seems to be all You'll allow me to do, I *will* go into private practice. If I starve, it's on Your head." I proceeded to sign a three-year lease on an office of my own and a one-year advertising contract with the Yellow Pages, all without a single client.

## The Twist in the Story

Within my first month of private practice, if it deserves the title, I was complaining at church one morning about an allergy-related cough I'd had for several years. A friend recommended that I go see a chiropractor who was also one of the leaders in our church, Dr. Brian Martin. My friend thought he might be able to help with the cough. I had never been to a chiropractor but decided to give it a try. Dr. Martin asked me about the history of the allergy and then, while I laid on my back on the adjustment table, he had me hold my right arm tightly against my side and said,

"Think about that morning cough." As I thought about it, he pulled on my arm and it went weak, even though I was intending to keep it strong. While pulling on the weak arm he quickly and lightly touched different points on my body until he found a spot that made my arm change from weak back to strong. Now at this point I had no idea what was going on, but it was over before I could object. He suggested that my body was indicating emotional roots to the allergy that had to do with events in my childhood. He specified ages and asked me what was going on during those times. He then had me place my hands on various organ points and points on my head while I thought about these supposed childhood emotions. He explained that these emotions might be "fueling" the cough and that we would "clear" them. He sent me off to watch the cough and see if it improved. It didn't.

But that seemingly insignificant office visit turned out to be the biggest surprise shift of my life. After finding out that I was a new therapist, Dr. Martin said, "You don't know it, but you really want to learn this." I replied, "No, I really don't. But thank you." I left that day confused and unsettled and not at all sure what had just happened. As I said, the cough did not improve, so I wasn't impressed with this suspicious treatment. I already had my theory of change well established. I didn't need an alternative mode of helping people. I was a newly trained Marriage and Family Therapist armed with a host of cognitive, behavioral modification and strategic tools in my bag. I was all set. But Dr. Martin (and looking back, God through him) wouldn't let me go. For an entire year Dr. Martin would bring up the subject on Sundays, ask me about my practice, and suggest that I learn "mind-body work". He promised I would love the results. I was polite, of course, but secretly thought he was exaggerating about those results. I didn't trust his tools spiritually. But *God's* relentless pursuit I could not politely dismiss.

As I have said, I was raised in belief. I have no consciousness of ever not knowing God. As a girl I not only had a constant faith but a real feeling of sweetness—of friendship with God. It feels awkward to put it in print, but I always felt like He not only loved me in the "Jesus loves the little children" sense but that He liked me. One of the ways I operated with God was to assume that if something crossed my path, unsolicited and repeatedly in a short period of time, it might be His prompting. He might be trying to tell me something. Sometimes it was and sometimes it wasn't. This time it lasted a year. Everywhere I looked, every book I read, every article that caught my eye, every old colleague I reconnected with all kept pointing to this idea of mind-body work. But this time it couldn't be God. We all know those things are New Age witchcraft, right? I ignored these promptings until they had just gone on so long that I couldn't help but respond. I agreed before the Lord to investigate it. That was all.

The next time Dr. Martin approached me about it, he asked me to go with him to a training course in Thought Field Therapy. This is a mind-body approach developed by Dr. Roger Callahan, who has a background both in psychology and chiropractic. I had heard of T.F.T. and was willing to see what was involved, since God was clearly pointing me in that direction for some reason. During that weekend-long training in Westminster, CO, Dr. Martin and I learned all about tapping sequences on the body called *algorithms* and how they could supposedly alleviate a broad range of psychological symptoms in a very short period of time. The sequences were simple; we memorized them by the end of the training. But I was already comfortable with my style of working with clients. I did not have a framework for integrating this sort of treatment into my practice. Subsequently, mind-body work got shelved for several months, until one night in Colorado Springs.

I had a contract with the Catholic diocese there to work with its clients. I had been traveling from Denver to Colorado Springs twice a week. One night I was closing up a marital case. We were having the typical closing session wrap-up: "It's been great working with you both", etc., when she mentioned how terrified she was about their upcoming plane trip. They were moving with the military to Hawaii. She had a paralyzing fear of flying. I remembered my T.F.T. training and how it is supposed to be able to clear phobias easily, so I took a chance and mentioned it. I wasn't very smooth in presentation. I said something really compelling like, "I just got trained in this new technique for phobias. I don't think it will work, but do you want to give it a try?" Surprisingly, she agreed. We started tapping.

I had her follow me through the simple sequence and report on her "SUD" levels—her "subjective units of distress"—after each round. Just like they were supposed to, her numbers kept lowering by increments of two. When she could no longer feel the fear, she said, "Well, that's great, but I'm not in a plane. If I was, I'm sure I would get the fear back." I concurred with her skepticism, but we had no way of testing the legitimacy of what we had just done, so I was about to pack things up when she said "Wait, I also have a fear of elevators. We could test that one." By now, having seen her awareness of the fear of flying dissipate like T.F.T. predicted it would, I was intrigued. We went through the same process with the elevator phobia and prepared to test our results. The three of us made our way around the building toward the elevator. As soon as it was physically within her sight, she crouched down toward the floor like a cat being led to the bathtub. Not promising.

We went through several more rounds of the algorithm while standing there until she was calm again. Then we walked over to the elevator. She was able to stand in front of it but wasn't able to go inside. We did a few more tapping rounds and continued this way. We repeated the tapping sequence for each progressive step until about 20 minutes later she was giggling quietly and taking 16 flights alone in the elevator while her husband and I stood dumfounded. He kept repeating, "I can't believe it. She's never ridden an elevator in our entire marriage. I can't believe it."

Needless to say I went home that night with a new interest in mind-body work. I had seen firsthand that it was effective. Clearly it worked, but I wanted to know *why* it worked. Did it work for the right reasons? You can get a Ouija board or a psychic to "work". But that doesn't mean those methods are of God. Working isn't proof of spiritual soundness. It took me a while longer to get convinced that these techniques could be working for the *right* reasons.

I sought God on it consistently and tried a little of it on some other well-established clients. I couldn't find anything in Scripture to directly support it and found some Scriptures that might even speak against it. My main question was this: how is this different from using a Ouija board or a psychic? Isn't this New Age? And yet as I continued to ask this of the Lord, He seemed to continue to draw me toward it by opening up more questions and possibilities in my heart. I asked for godly counsel. I tried to find literature speaking to this issue. There was almost none. There was plenty of literature about New Age practices but none discussing these tools specifically and whether or not they were outside of God's spiritual boundaries. They discussed things like paranormal abilities that were clearly ungodly, but they didn't address the connection between mind and body and how it might work. I could find no literature discussing the theoretical energy system in the body from a believing perspective. I just continued to ask God and trust that He would make things clear to me. I employed an old strategy I had decided on as a teenager.

I remember when I was probably 16 or so, having a daunting decision I was trying to make (I don't even remember now what it was), I realized that I could never really know God's specific lead. I could ask and have a hunch, but I didn't hear from God like our biblical forerunners, so in essence it was always a shot in the dark. This realization seemed paralyzing. It struck me that believers often respond to this dilemma in one of three ways: many live like practical agnostics. They mean well when they say, "Jesus is Lord", but they don't really involve God in their decisions beyond attempting to line them up with His general principles for holiness. There seems to be little assumption that God is personal or available to us in any real way. Those who do attempt to involve God can end up living life like the Christian version of horoscope-followers. They ask God for intervention, direction, or confirmation and then attribute every little stub of the toe or great parking place to "the sovereignty of God". Others who cannot land in either camp can just get stuck in paralysis, unable to make significant moves or changes in their lives because of never being able to confidently know the will of God. I decided at that optimistic age that if God was who He says He is—passionate about our lives, intimately near, and perfectly wise—then surely there must be a better way for a believer to navigate life.

I remember saying to God something like this, "OK, here's the deal. You are trustworthy to answer my prayers and guide my life, so when I have a decision to make, I'm going to surrender it to You completely. As well as I know how, I will give it up to You and open my heart to whatever You decide. And then I'm going to ask You to direct my heart—to align my heart with Yours on the subject. From then on I'm going to assume that the direction my heart leans is *from You* and move on it. I'm going to trust that if I'm wrong, You will redirect me." Simple but practical. It's the only way I could come up with to move the idea of following God's lead into reality without a divine fortune cookie showing up every time there was a decision to make.

I took on that style of life navigation then; God honored my stretch in trust. I was fairly established in this way of operating with God by the time I got to the question of Energy Psychology. So I employed my tactic. I laid the whole issue at His feet and said I would not move forward with it unless I got clearance and confirmation from Him. This was not a life direction I could take lightly. I had to *know* He was leading it. I had to *know* these tools were of Him before I not only took this path myself but brought decades of fellow believing clients along with me. It's one thing to take a risk for yourself. It's quite another to lead others into it. There was simply too much at stake. This was no casual decision. I was not up for a millstone around my neck.

### Out on a Limb

What happened increasingly over the next year or so was that my heart not only kept being drawn to these tools but also drawn to the very questions they create. I became more and more gripped with both the problems and the potentials of this field if approached from a biblical perspective. God seemed to keep reminding me of the simple fact that His creation is good . . . all of it. He was drawing me into a deeply redemptive posture of heart. He wasn't giving me answers per se. He was giving me passion.

Many small examples of confirmation appeared along the way, but I'll explain the main turning point. A few years after training in Thought Field Therapy I had also become trained in Neuro-Emotional Technique. This is a mind-body protocol designed within the chiropractic community. It was the tool Dr. Martin was using in our first meeting. A significant contribution made by this protocol is that of "muscle testing", which we will get into later. Muscle testing is for most Christians, and was for me, the most difficult sticking point in the mind-body world. To say that the body and mind are affecting one another is no big leap and is not particularly theologically challenging. The trouble starts in the ways the field of Energy Psychology taps into that connection and alters it. The theory behind the practice of muscle testing is that a muscle will respond to energetic shifts that go off in the body. Subsequently, it is a way that the body can respond to ideas or substances in a "yes/no" style. Again the question was "how is this different from a Ouija board or a psychic or what Scripture calls *divination*?"

I was in session one evening with a well-established talk therapy client. We were spending our last 15 minutes of session experimenting with Thought Field Therapy (the first of three Energy Psychology tools I would eventually incorporate into the Splankna protocol). This was the way I got my feet wet during the confirmation stage, when I was still not entirely convinced these tools were of God. There were a few believing clients with whom I had a solid rapport who were interested in pursuing the questions with me. They would indulge me in "practicing" during the last few minutes of session. Bathing this investigation in prayer and asking God to lead me into whatever was really true, this was one of the main modes I used to pursue Him in it during those early days. He was nearer during those times than I had previously experienced. Most believers know what it's like to be reading a Scripture you've read a thousand times and all of a sudden one phrase stands out, as if the Holy Spirit has just shined a spotlight on it so that you will notice. Those kinds of moments were rampant during these times, both in confirmation and in correction when I would think or try something that was out of line.

One evening, I don't remember how the idea came up (looking back I'm sure it was a prompting by the Holy Spirit), but somehow I ended up asking my client, through a muscle test, if there was spiritual warfare bothering with her and blocking our work. Her body responded in the affirmative. I had no idea what to do with that. My background did not prepare me for this. We don't have demons in the Church of Christ. I had absolutely no education or experience in dealing with warfare even in an abstract sense, much less present in my office. I literally looked up to heaven and said, "What do I do now?" I knew my biblical example was simply to tell the presence to leave in Jesus' Name. So I said simply, "In Jesus' Name, leave." I retested; the presence seemed to be gone. I sat back surprised and feeling a little proud of myself when suddenly I had one of those moments where it feels like God zips your head open and pours in a whole new way of thinking.

He reminded me of the story in the Gospels when the Pharisees are accusing Jesus of casting out demons by the power of Beelzebub. Jesus basically replied that that would not be logical. Satan would not cast out Satan. "*A house divided against itself would fall*" (Luke 11:17, see also Mt. 12:25). He showed me the simple truth that if these tools were *inherently* demonic, the enemy would not allow me to use them to find him and cast him out. That house would be divided against itself and would fall. After so many other subtle moments and styles of confirmation, that moment was so clearly given by the Holy Spirit that it was the final turning point for me. I agreed before the Lord that I would obey Him and pursue this perilous field of Energy Psychology. But that decision brought on more questions than answers.

What would it look like to utilize these tools without incorporating New Age philosophies? Where were the spiritual boundaries to keep one safe from warfare? How could I present this work apologetically? How would I account for the absence of direct scriptural references to it? Were all Energy Psychology practices endorsed by God, or were there only a few? I embarked on the next season—pressing into God with these questions, searching the Word, and asking for accountability and intercession from trusted fellow believers.

# CHAPTER 2

# The Basics of Energy

*"One's mind, once stretched by a new idea, never regains its original dimensions." —Oliver Wendell Holmes*

*"There are only two ways to live your life. One is as though nothing is a miracle. The other is as though everything is a miracle." —Albert Einstein*

In order to discuss Energy Psychology we need to define what we mean by *energy*.

## The Alternative World

Let's start at the beginning. Because of emerging scientific findings on the role of physiology in emotional health, new fields of alternative medicine and psychology have been in development for several decades. Alternative medicine differs from allopathic medicine in that it assumes that health is found in physiological balance and that the body naturally pushes for this balance. The change agent of healing therefore is to support the body in restoring that balance. Western allopathic medicine functions largely on the model of opposing symptoms rather than supporting balance. Both views have deep merit. Similarly, alternative psychology employs a very different theory of change than traditional psychology. It asserts that a person's physiology is an integral part of their psychological health and that change is supported by the incorporation of the body into therapy. Alternative psychology assumes that behavioral and emotional change requires insight *and* some form of physiological shift beyond the mere adjustment of brain chemistry through medication. There is currently a wide mix of therapeutic modalities that attempt to integrate mind and body more holistically.

A simple and well-known example is aromatherapy. Neuroscience has discovered the interface between the olfactory system in the body and mood disorders.[1] Scent affects people emotionally. The aromatherapist, therefore, begins with traditional therapeutic insight into the client problem and then introduces different natural aromas intended to positively affect client emotional states. It is theorized that the body receives the scent. The scent acts upon the emotion center in the brain and helps change symptoms like depression and anxiety. Under the larger umbrella of alternative or mind-body psychology are treatments that work with the body's "energy system" in order to facilitate change. Before we discuss energy as it relates to psychology, let's clarify what we mean by the word.

## What Is Energy?

*Energy* is the term that science is currently using to describe the cause of the movement found at the smallest level of life. It's a metaphor for whatever it is that causes things at the smallest level of creation to be in motion. The earliest recorded reference to some kind of subtle energy or life force was 5000 B.C. in India, where it was called *prana*. In Japan and

China it is called *qi* (pronounced "chee"). Pythagoras called it *vital energy* in 500 B.C. In Hawaii it is called *mana*.[2] *Qi* can be defined as "the breath or vital energy of which all things are composed".[3] It is said to flow through the body and require harmony and balance in order to facilitate health and long life.

All things are made up of atoms. Everything. Atoms contain electrons and protons, which are made up of particles. We can't see atoms yet (much less particles), because they are too small. We have yet to develop tools that can allow the naked eye to see things at that level. But through theorizing and experimentation, physicists have come to know at least enough about these atoms to split them and create Hiroshima.

Quantum physics is the study of matter at the sub-atomic level (meaning smaller than atoms). Since we cannot yet see things at that level, the entire scientific field is technically theoretical. But don't let that fool you. To put it as simply as possible, quantum physicists say to themselves "We think it works this way. And if it does, then when we perform function 'A', result 'B' should occur." So they take their theory of cause and effect to the lab. When they try it out, it works. When they do "A" (whatever that may be in the moment), "B" happens, confirming their suspicion about how things probably function down at that miniscule level. In fact, "B" happens so reliably that quantum physics is just as legitimate scientifically as Newtonian or classical physics that tells us how to navigate to the moon.

Quantum physics suggests that at this "quantum level", or the smallest level of creation, all matter is in motion. All of the atoms are buzzing. The theoretical particles inside the atoms are also in motion. Nothing is as solid as it seems. Everything is moving. At the smallest level, all things from a rock to a brain to a Ritz cracker seem to be made up of the same buzzing particles. What *keeps* them buzzing is what we're calling *"energy"*. I use quotations with the word *energy* at this point because it is really just used metaphorically. Scientifically speaking, we don't really know what makes the particles move. It is not energy in the strict traditional sense but figuratively. It is elementally dynamic—in apparently self-propelled constant motion. So *energy* has become the catchword for this force.

## The Great Unknown

This level of creation is mysterious. The subatomic world operates in all sorts of bizarre ways. Our current models, though reliable, are still insufficient. For instance, there is Heisenberg's Uncertainty Principle.[4] It shows that the position of a subatomic particle can be known and its speed/velocity can be known, but they cannot be known at the same time. Further, particles seem to be capable of being in two different spaces at the same time. If you split one and put half of it in L.A. and the other half in New York and vibrate one of them, the other will also vibrate. These particles even seem to travel from point A to point B without crossing the distance in between. Mysterious.

Scientist Fritjov Capra describes it this way: "Quantum theory has thus demolished the classical concepts of solid objects and of strictly deterministic laws of nature. At the subatomic level, the solid material objects of classical physics dissolve into wave-like patterns of probabilities, and these patterns, ultimately, do not represent probabilities of things, but rather probabilities of interconnections . . .. It shows that we cannot decompose the world into independently existing smallest units. As we penetrate into matter, nature does not show us any isolated basic building blocks, but rather appears as a complicated web of relations between various parts of the whole."[5]

The most decisive property of subatomic particles that relates to our discussion is that *they cannot be observed with objectivity*. Let's look further into the Heisenberg Uncertainty Principle. Quantum physicists realize that the very act of observation significantly affects the particles. Subsequently there is no way to objectively observe them, because the observation *itself* has changed them. The particles will be in a particular state, but as soon as we go to observe them in any way, our observation changes their state. Attention itself seems to affect the particles. Our focus is powerful. This discovery has spawned the "power of intention" revolution within New Age.

Until the discovery of the quantum level, we operated within Newtonian or classical physics. In that world, everything is either a particle or a wave. In order to measure a particle or wave in Newtonian (macro) physics, you need two pieces of information: position and velocity. If you have these two pieces of information, you can predict the trajectory of that particle or wave. If we know the original position of a cannon ball and its velocity (the combination of speed and mass), we can accurately predict where it will land. Loosely the same applies to all things. Subsequently, Newtonian physics, which reigned since Galileo, postulated that if one could know the position and velocity of all the particles in the universe, one could predict all future outcomes. This led to a deterministic worldview and the scientific revolution. Man began to see the universe as a Swiss watch; all events were scripted by predictable measurement.

But the discovery of the quantum level destroyed Newton's watch. Things are radically different there. For instance, at the quantum level, you cannot measure either position or velocity without destructively altering the other or making it unknowable. You can know the position of a particle. You can know its velocity. But you cannot know them at the same time. You can only know one or the other. Therefore, we cannot predict *anything* at the quantum level. The motion of all things seems to be random, capricious.

Einstein assumed that this was just a function of our ignorance and that as our tools grow sharper we will eventually be able to measure both factors at the same time and reliably predict again. He is famous for saying "God does not play dice with the universe." Others, such as Christian astronomer and scientist Hugh Ross, disagree. Ross argues, "It is not that

37

the Heisenberg Uncertainty Principle disproves the principle of causality, but simply that the causality is hidden from human investigation."[6] He means that while God does play a causal role in the cosmos (not random dice-throwing), His mechanisms are hidden from us. They are purposefully left mysterious.

## Weighty Intention

Now there are several theories about *why* we cannot observe the quantum particles clearly. One is that light particles themselves are larger than the quantum particles, so that when we shine light on them to observe them, the light literally knocks them off course (assuming they had a course to begin with, which is debatable). Another theory is that the consciousness of the observer knocks the particles out of position (assuming they had a position to begin with, which is also debatable).

This second theory applies to our discussion. *It seems scientifically possible that the observation or intention of human sentience affects the particles*. The truth is that although the theories in quantum physics are remarkably reliable, we do not yet know exactly why. If thought does affect matter, we do not have an explainable mechanism for that, only the empirical observation that it appears to be so.

At the macro/Newtonian level of physics, everything is either a wave or a particle. But at the quantum level, things seem to exist in a state of potential. They can either be a wave or a particle, depending on many variables. When we observe them, the wave-like function collapses and one particle state is actualized. Heisenberg himself says, "Natural science does not simply describe and explain nature, it describes nature as it is exposed to our method of questioning."[7]

J. C. Polkinghorn, author of "Quarks, Chaos and Christianity", says that working within quantum mechanics is like being shown a magnificent palace and then being told that "no one is quite sure whether its foundations rest on bedrock or shifting sand."[8] Considering that Polkinghorn in all of his scholarship has yet to unravel these mysteries, we are going to let quantum mechanism rest here. For now, on to the body.

## Energy in the Body

This energy we're talking about is thought to be keeping these illusive particles buzzing not only at the smallest level of all creation in general but inside the human body as well. It is thought to be elemental to our being alive. The theory on body energy goes something like this: It seems to move through the body along micro-thin pathways called "meridians". The concept of energy meridians in the body was first developed through traditional Chinese medicine.

Energy pathways seem to correlate to physical functioning on all levels. They pass through organs and tissues and support all of our bodily operations. They are named based on the body systems they relate to, for example, liver/gallbladder meridian, lung/large intestine meridians, etc. Acupuncture points are spots along these meridian pathways that are thought to correlate to specific bodily functions and to overall health.

Until recently, the existence of the meridian system was purely speculative, an almost metaphoric subtle energy network. However, there is some recent research suggesting evidence of its physical existence. Acupuncture sites (the same sites used in Energy Psychology) have qualities that make them unique. One of those qualities is a difference in electrical conductivity compared with surrounding tissue. Ordinarily the acupuncture sites have a significantly lower electrical resistance compared to surrounding skin locations, suggesting that they may be more receptive in some way to stimulation.[9]

Several decades ago, Kim Bong Han, a Korean scientist, discovered that the meridians are a network of microtubules. Studying rabbits and dogs, he found a vast network of microtubules, each about one-third the diameter of a human hair. These pass through the walls of veins and arteries as well as around and through various organs. He also discovered circulating within the microtubules a rich concentrate of DNA, RNA, and a variety of neuropeptides and other chemical messengers that are also known to wash over the brain.[10]

More physical evidence of the meridian pathways can be found in photographs taken at University of Paris Hospital in 1985-86. Physician and researchers Jean Claude Darras and Pierre de Vernejoul injected radioactive isotopes into meridian and non-meridian sites. At the meridian location, the fluid flow is coherent and can be traced along a known meridian pathway; at the non-meridian site it dissipates locally.[11] This simple test suggests that these energy meridian pathways do in fact exist in the body and that the isotopes are naturally drawn to trace them.

University of California at Irvine physicist Zang-Hee Cho, Ph.D., is credited with inventing the prototype of the positron emission tomograph (PET) scan and was a pioneer of magnetic resonance imaging (MRI). When his back was injured some years ago, he found relief through acupuncture. As an inquiring scientist, he began using MRI technology to explore how acupuncture works. He found that the MRI was able to identify the effects of an acupuncture treatment administered at the site of the little toe upon blood flow to the brain, where no direct nerve, blood, or other connection existed. Dr. Cho's findings were published in the spring of 1998, Proceedings of the National Academy of Sciences, providing further evidence of the existence of energy systems in the body.[12]

Our Eastern global neighbors were the first to theorize about these energy pathways. Most Eastern medicine and philosophy take for granted these energy meridians and assume that the proper flow of energy in the body is directly related to all aspects of health. If you have a knee that keeps locking up and you go to an acupuncturist for treatment, he will place needles along the energy meridian pathway that is thought to correlate to the function of that knee. The assumption is that the energy flow to and around the knee is blocked or moving backwards and that the needles will re-draw the energy current back into the correct flow. If the flow of energy is corrected, the knee is supported in healing. There are many different types of treatments both in Eastern and Western culture that are used to work with this body energy to help alleviate physical symptoms. Acupuncture and chiropractic are the most well-known.

At the smallest level of creation, everything is in motion—everything in creation, everything in the body. The word *energy* is used metaphorically to describe whatever it is that keeps everything moving. The way these tiny particles move and the types of behavior they exhibit is mysterious and so far unexplainable. Energy Psychology and Energy Healing techniques aim at manipulating this energy in different styles, in order to facilitate change and restore wholeness.

The quantum level is enigmatic and startling. Isn't it wonderful that God has given us such an exquisite setting? Isn't it fun? In Galileo's day, the most brilliant scientific minds alive believed that the sun rotated around the earth. We will certainly continue to enjoy the shock and adventure of searching an unsearchable creation.

# Chapter 3

# Energy in Psychology

*"The significant problems we face cannot be solved
at the same level of thinking we were at
when we created them." —Albert Einstein*

O ur next step is to discuss how this quantum energy relates to psychology. *Energy Psychology* refers to the field of treatment protocols that seek to alleviate psychological symptoms via biomeridian manipulation. How's that for losing you? It assumes that the energy that permeates our bodies and runs through our meridians is related to our emotional functioning as well as our physical functioning. Put more simply, Energy Psychology uses the body's energy system to help heal emotional problems.

Such treatments are quickly on the rise. Energy Psychology protocols are being utilized not only in a wide array of mental-health settings but also in disaster-relief organizations, HMO's, and V.A. hospitals. They were used at the Oklahoma City bombings where Charles Figley from the Department of Veteran Affairs is quoted as saying that "EP is rapidly proving itself to be among the most powerful psychological interventions available to disaster-relief workers for helping the survivors as well as the workers themselves." The American Psychological Association describes Energy Psychology as "a new discipline that has been receiving attention due to its speed and effectiveness with difficult cases".[13]

Unfortunately, this very "speed" has worked against the field in some respects. Early claims of the fast pace and accuracy of these tools were exaggerated by enthusiastic practitioners. Exaggerations naturally illegitimized discoveries that were already too easy to dismiss because they are threatening to established psychology. Another dock against Energy Psychology is its lack of traditional research. Other than E.M.D.R., Energy Psychology tools tend to have little to point to in the way of clinical trials. Considering that we have yet to design a tool to observe the energetic level, Energy Psychology does not lend itself well to standard double-blind tests. The best research proof to be found is anecdotal from client-reported outcomes. [Generally we assume that the western medical world has their research ducks in a row and that "proof" in the holistic world pales in comparison. However, Tulane University Professor Dr. James Carter points out a surprising reality. In his article on chelation therapy he references a report from a branch of Congress (the office of Technology Assessment) revealing that only an unbelievable "10-20% of procedures currently used in western medical practice have been shown effective by controlled trials."[14]] Thirdly, Energy Psychology's legitimacy is weakened because it is not perfectly consistent. The same protocol applied to clients with the same symptom will have varying results.

Weaknesses admitted, Energy Psychology is a burgeoning new field, ripe with potential. Here we will discuss its basic assumptions. The first is that our bodies seem to store all the emotions we experience in our lives like electrical charges. When we feel intense emotion, the body and the subconscious mind seem to hold something like an imprint of them—like an energetic residue. At any given moment in a person's life, it is as if they are carrying their entire life experience in their body's hard drive. The body carries these emotions and memories, both positive and negative. It seems that everything we think or feel has its own unique kind of energetic signature resonance. If you were to observe the body in any emotional state, upon investigation you would find that the current emotion is manifested in a particular brain chemistry, neurological design, and energetic signature in the body. This is assumed to be true for any thought or emotion. When I feel angry, my brain chemistry is matching the chemical balance for anger. When I'm aroused, my neuro-networks are firing in a specific pattern that matches that state.

Emotions also seem to be stored in the body at an energetic level. They are stored in particular places called "meridian points" or "alarm points". The body seems to have a well-ordered cataloging system for these emotions. For instance anger will be consistently stored in the Liver alarm point, grief will be stored in the Lung point, and so on. Recent research done by Candace Pert, described in her book "Molecules of Emotion",[15] indicates that there is indeed more physiology to emotion than we have previously thought. From her exploration in microbiology, she explains that every cell in the body is covered in tiny receptors to which only specific molecules can attach. These molecules such as hormones and proteins (or peptides) function as tiny pieces of information in the body. They affect every organ, system, and function. It is thought that this discovery begins to explain why embarrassing emotions can cause the pulse to race and the face to flush. Body and emotion are in tight communication.

This translates into our psychological symptoms because the negative emotions that we store physiologically become a kind of fuel for dysfunction. Every time something happens in my life that reminds my body or my subconscious of a previous trauma, it is as if an old file gets activated and my reaction is exaggerated.

For instance, let's say I was in a terrible car accident. I might feel intense fear, shock, and powerlessness. My body stores those emotions from that trauma. I carry them into the rest of my life. Years later I might still have a phobia of driving or of being a passenger in a car. Whenever I buckle into the passenger seat, my system as a whole says, "What do we have filed on this experience?" Up comes all of that stored trauma. When those emotions surface, even if I'm not consciously thinking of the original trauma, my body may experience a panic attack.

For another example, if my father died when I was young, I may have felt deep abandonment and grief. As an adult it may still be unusually difficult for me to relate to my father-in-law. Conversations with him trigger those old stored emotions from my father; the pain surfaces.

We know this intuitively. All of us have instances in normal life where if we could freeze a moment in time, we could recognize in our conscious mind that this situation probably calls for a subtle emotional reaction, but our *automatic* reaction is much more intense and irrational. I should be mildly irritated right now, but instead I'm shaking with rage because this moment has called up an old, associated trauma.

Now so far we're not differing from the basic assumptions in traditional psychology. Ever since Freud it has been assumed that our psychological symptoms come from our past. We know intuitively that our emotional issues and imbalances are rooted in our past traumas. The question is, what do you do about it? How do you heal? That's where Energy Psychology differs. It presents a radically different "theory of change".

## Theories of Change

My hands were shaky as I handed Dr. Hinson the videotape. It contained the raw footage of my first counseling session as a student therapist. He was my supervisor for this semester in graduate school. In just a moment he would slide the tape into the VCR (yes, the VCR). My supervision group would get to watch my debut performance. I hadn't watched it yet myself; I was nervous. I squirmed through the agonizing viewing, sure that my classmates must be appalled at my incompetence. It seemed like hours passed as we sat and watched my little display of therapeutic angst, but it did finally come to an end and I slumped back into my chair, awaiting the critical onslaught. My classmates said nothing, probably because their videos were coming next and they were lost in their own anticipatory anxiety. Dr. Hinson turned to me with the last response I expected. He said simply, "That was great, Sarah, but what's your *theory of change?*" My theory of change? I was lucky to avoid a panic attack during that opening hour and he's asking me about my theory of change?

Looking back now, I know exactly what Dr. Hinson was thinking. Without a solid, workable theory of change, the therapeutic process is no different than a chat over coffee with a nosey neighbor. He was making sure his progeny faced this from the beginning. When the psychological community asks you for your "theory of change", they are asking what you understand the actual change agent to be in the therapeutic process. For instance, do you believe that change is caused by the relationship itself that is established between the therapist and the client? Or does change occur when the client gains insight into his behaviors? Is it cathartic emotional experiences that cause change? The traditional list of therapeutic theories of change includes re-learning problematic behavior patterns, changing thought habits, assumptions, and beliefs, re-narrating one's history in a more productive light, and many other cognitive, strategic, and analytically oriented constructs. The assumption is that if a person employs these tools of self-mastery, symptoms can be relieved.

If you are doing therapy, you are working within a particular theory of change, whether you realize it or not. If you're a Cognitive/Behavioralist, you're bringing about change by helping the client recognize and re-train thought patterns that are assumed to underlie behavior. If you're a Freudian therapist, you're helping the client change by gaining insight into their childhood associations and projections. You're utilizing the transference process to reframe their interactional patterns with authority and nurture figures. If you're a Solution-Focused therapist, you're fostering change through identifying the successful behavior patterns the client already has in place in other areas of life and replicating them in the problematic areas. There are many more examples like these. No matter what kind of therapist you are, you're working under some theory of change—some basic belief about what *causes* a psychological problem and what *causes* people to change.

Theories of change explain why it is that the energetic healing modalities have come almost exclusively from Eastern philosophical roots. The connection comes from the philosophy of healing behind alternative/energetic thinking as opposed to allopathic (western medicine) thinking. Again, there are many good books devoted to this subject alone, but in brief: allopathy proposes that when a symptom occurs, physical or emotional, the practitioner must oppose the symptom in order to stop it. This usually looks like some form of drugs or surgery (which, it must be said, are invaluable when necessary). The alternative thought process is based on balance and the human system's ability to heal itself. The alternative practitioner assumes that the individual is thoroughly systemic, that all of its parts are interrelated and interdependent, and that balance is synonymous with health. This paradigm was born and developed predominantly in the East.

As I worked my way through my graduate program, my own theory of change was evolving into a hodge-podge of multi-generational insight and systemic restructuring. But in essence, I came at client problems assuming they could be *reasoned* into changing.

One of the most excruciating parts of graduate school was "live supervision". This was a specially designed torture where the professors and fellow students would observe a live therapy session through the one-way mirror. You have to understand—as a student-therapist you basically have no idea what you're doing. You feel like a fraud in session; like at any minute you could pull off your rubber mask and be exposed as completely useless. So it's especially challenging to be observed during this display by anyone who really does know what he or she is doing.

One Thursday morning I was in the throes of one of these live supervision sessions with a married couple, when Dr. Parish beeped in. He told me to come out and meet him in the hall. When I did, he passed me by, went into the room with my clients, and took over the session. Humiliating. Afterward he pulled me aside, sat me down, and gave me some of the best supervision wisdom I'll probably ever receive: "Sarah, insight doesn't produce change."

He explained to me that my strength was being able to observe a client system and discern what was wrong with the structure of their interactions. He said what I was doing was *explaining* this to clients. I was illuminating for them the details of where their feedback loops operated, the secondary gain involved, the crucial imbalances and false beliefs at work, and anything else pertinent to their case. The clients generally loved this approach. It was popular. They loved the opportunity to navel-gaze; everyone went home happy after sessions, filled with new insights into themselves and their symptoms. I was brilliant; they were "helped". The problem was that all of this wonderful insight did not produce *change*. They would come back the next week in exactly the same predicaments; we would go through the whole circus again. My theory of change wasn't *changing* anything!

As a general rule, clients don't usually seem to change as much as we therapists hope they will. We all dream of gorgeous relational transformations, marriages restored, addictions broken, fears abated, and a deeply satisfied gut at the end of every work day, fraught with the knowledge that the world is a better place because of our contribution. But the reality looks more like one of my supervisors' statements while I was working at Boulder County Mental Health: "You need to lower your standards of 'success' with clients." This was her answer to my feelings of deep frustration and powerlessness in working with day-treatment adolescents . . . lower your expectations; you won't be so disappointed. This was my first real attempt as a therapist since grad school. Her answer was profoundly disheartening. I never could bring myself to embrace that point of view.

But people *want* to change, right? Consciously, yes. Every client gets comfortable on the couch and explains that they are dealing with such-and-such symptom and want it resolved. No one ever woke up on a Tuesday morning and said to themselves, "I think I'd like to be clinically depressed for the next six years." The conscious mind *never* chooses symptoms. Think about it for a moment. Consciously, every human being chooses health, vitality, wholeness, joy. But clearly something else in us chooses symptoms because they're alive and well and causing us various problems. Due to this unfortunate human state, even the most brilliant therapist has a limitation. Their main tool in therapy is the client's conscious mind; that is not where the problem typically resides. Consciously they've already told you they want to be whole. The problem lies in the *subconscious* mind. Most of the traditional therapeutic tools do not access or treat that level.

The therapy world does have a few tricks up its collective sleeve to access this subconscious symptom center. The best-known in my opinion are hypnosis and the strategic therapy of Chloe Madanes and Jay Haley.[16] Dr. Parish explained the latter option to me that afternoon. He explained that although I was great at offering the clients insight into their issues, insight isn't enough. The effective therapist must *use* his insight about the client problem to create situations inside and outside of the therapy room that interrupt rutted behavior patterns and force the client system to create new ones. This gets at the subconscious. Terrific, but much more easily said than done. For those of you who are skilled at this approach, I applaud you. You should know, you're brilliant. But the rest of us with average-sized brains need a more user-friendly pipeline into the subconscious.

Every experienced therapist knows her—the lovely 20-something, despondent over the repeated pain in her romantic life. Over and over she has experienced the same thing. Maybe she is attracted to addicts or men who lie, but whatever the pattern, she is exhausted. You've given her all the insight, support, scolding, affirmation, and homework assignments you can possibly give. You've explained how she chooses these men because she was abandoned by her father or abused by her stepmother and never came to really know her worth. But despite all of your valiant efforts, here she is again. She's "Marie" in *When Harry Met Sally*. "You're right . . . I know you're right." And consciously she *does* know. But nothing changes. There are times when change cannot occur through conscious effort. If our conscious minds were running the show independently, we would all be in much better shape. But unfortunately, we're all Marie in some area of life.

Rather than trying to beat the subconscious mind into submission through the dutiful conscious mind (which most clients have already tried *ad nauseam* on their own), Energy Psychology goes in through the body door. The theory of change in Energy Psychology is energetic adjustment. It uses what the Splankna protocol calls "Circuitry + Intention".

## Circuitry + Intention

Through the first few years of my exploration into the field, I realized that all the different Energy Psychology protocols (20 or so) had one thing in common. They all combined two simple elements in some fashion or another. They each had their unique way of manipulating the earlier-introduced meridian system of energy (Circuitry) while having the client focus his or her thoughts on something specific (Intention). Since the body is carrying the traumatic emotional "fuel" behind our symptoms, Energy Psychology comes in through this body door to create change physiologically, instead of through insight and the conscious mind.

It appears to work this way: When you touch, tap, activate with a needle, etc., a meridian point on the body while thinking of the particular emotion that is thought to be stored there, it facilitates the body's ability to resolve that stored emotional charge on a physiological level. For instance, if I touch the meridian spot on my body where a charge of anger is stored from a previous trauma while thinking about that anger, my body is able to resolve that energetic emotional charge on a physiological level and the "fuel" behind my symptom is reduced—energetic "circuitry" combined with client intention. That is Energy Psychology's theory of change— identify where the body is storing that emotional charge and activate that point while thinking about the emotion. In varying degrees, resolution occurs.

Even after all these years it still sounds a bit preposterous to me. Crazier still is the fact that we don't even know exactly *how* or *why* this works yet. It very reliably does work; we just don't have any tools to observe what is literally happening in the body. We discussed earlier that we cannot see "energy". We can see through client report and behavior that the emotional charge behind a symptom does seem to be alleviated through this "circuitry + intention" technique, but we don't have a way to watch or measure what is literally happening in the body-mind connection. We only see its results. We hear the client say with surprise, "That old anger reaction just doesn't seem to be coming up any more." But we can't watch the mechanism in action. It's like gravity. We knew that if you dropped an apple, it would fall to the ground, long before we could explain why from a scientific rationale. At this point in history we are at one of those stages again . . . where we can observe clearly that something is effective, but we aren't sure *how* or *why* yet. The mechanism of how the combination of touch and thought affect the body or symptoms is still mysterious—as mysterious as everything else at the quantum energetic level.

When it comes to the *how* part, the purely physiological element does have some clarity. A growing body of scientific evidence suggests that when meridian points are stimulated *in combination with specific intention*, a number of beneficial physical results occur, such as the increased production of opioids, serotonin, and GABA, the regulation of cortisol, pain reduction, slowed heart rate, decreased anxiety, shut-off of the fight or flight response, and an increased sense of calm. However, these benefits are not found when stimulation of the acupuncture points is applied generically, without focused intention.[17] Circuitry without intention does not seem to have the same effect.

What happens to the emotion? Different schools of thought have their theories. Some think it's like letting go of a helium balloon. The emotional charge just lifts off the body somehow. Others think it's more like a thought "field" of some kind with a glitch in it that gets smoothed out. But no one really knows. What we observe is that when you combine the energetic "circuitry + intention", the strong emotion that the body was holding onto from some previous trauma seems to be resolved, like deleting a file. The person can no longer access that strong emotion. When focusing on the trauma that previously triggered an intense emotional charge, they now feel calm or neutral. And that neutrality is typically permanent. The memory of the event does not change, but the strong emotional charge attached to the memory is cleared out. The client would have to go back to that age and experience that trauma again in order to "get back" the emotions. Something seems to happen in the body through this combination of circuitry and intention that permanently uncouples the emotions from the trauma.

The simplest example is a phobia. Let's say that when I was 5 years old, I fell off the bunk bed onto the hardwood floor and broke my arm; ever since then I've had a fear of heights. Now my adult logic tells me that a fear of heights is irrational. Consciously I know that I'm safe to walk over to the four-story window and look down. But when I do it's as if my computer system says, "What do we have on file for '*height*'? What are the associations?" And up to my screen comes the entire stored trauma from that childhood event (and any others that are related to height traumas). When the memory is originally stored, it is kept in full emotional intensity. When it is triggered, no matter how many years later, it comes up at that same full intensity as if it is happening again. So in this moment in front of the window my body trembles in fear, while my logic says, "That's not rational." As we've said before, all of us have many of these experiences in our lives. These are times when if we could freeze-frame a moment and step out of it, we would recognize that on a scale of 1 to 10, this moment calls for about a 2, but I'm at about a 9.5, so what's going on with me? What's going on is that the moment triggered some older trauma and up to my screen came not only this moment but the old one, too, so I overreacted, whether in anger, pain, or fear, etc.

Again, traditional psychology would explain the correlation between experiences of trauma and current symptoms in much the same way. The difference here is what to do about it. Unfortunately no amount of insight into this connection between the past and the present will stop the automatic reaction from going off. I cannot will myself out of the phobic reaction. If I'm the typical client in treatment, I have tried that over and over. Others have tried as well to reason me out of my irrational phobia, but to no avail. Through more traditional therapeutic methods I can get very useful work done. With my conscious effort I can get better over time at *managing* those trauma emotions when they rise up. I can employ self-soothing techniques, moderate my breathing, re-narrate the original trauma, remind myself of the rational facts that can calm me down. Or I can spend a great deal of time and emotional effort avoiding the circumstances that trigger the unwanted responses. But I cannot, by conscious effort, prevent the emotional automatic reaction from happening in the first place. Here is where Energy Psychology comes in with a completely different approach.

Through that combination of "circuitry + intention," what Energy Psychology aims to do is *clear* those 5-year-old trauma emotions out of my "height file" completely, not by erasing the memory itself but by neutralizing the emotional charge that is attached to the memory and stored in the body, so that there isn't anything to manage anymore. As a result, when I walk to that same four-story window and my eye sees the height, my system will still say, "What do we have in the 'height file'?" But now the file is cleaned out; there is no strong emotional reaction. I stand at the same window that has always given me a panic attack and quietly note that no triggers are going off. That old, familiar, strong reaction simply does not occur.

Now the "why" part of this tool's effectiveness is no trifle. In fact, it's crucial. As believers we must ask why it works. We cannot afford to be casual here, because potentially it could work for the wrong reasons. That would preclude us from using these tools. We *have* to ask why, and we will, once we've laid all the mechanisms on the table.

Over the years I developed what is now the Splankna Therapy protocol. Its elements have roots in the following established mind-body schools of thought, though it does not follow any of their protocols specifically. If the founders of any of these three schools were to sit in on a Splankna session, I am sure they would recognize the commonalities.

## Thought Field Therapy

This amazing effect of combining touch and thought was discovered by several different enterprising individuals, all within approximately a 10-year period. Today about 20 recognized Energy Psychology protocols currently are in use in the field, most initially developed around 10 to 20 years ago. The Splankna Therapy protocol utilizes elements from three of them: Thought Field Therapy, Neuro-Emotional Technique, and E.M.D.R. (Eye Movement Desensitization and Reprocessing).

The first Energy Psychology protocol in which I was trained, as I already mentioned, was Thought Field Therapy or T.F.T. About 20 years ago Dr. Roger Callahan, who had a Ph.D. in Clinical Psychology and also a background in chiropractic, was working with a client who had a paralyzing phobia of water. She was so profoundly terrified that she hadn't showered in years. She had to take sponge baths. He was frustrated with his lack of progress with her and was experimenting one day. Since he knew about the Meridian System of Energy through his chiropractic experience, he wondered if meridian points related to emotions. In the spirit of pushing the envelope, he had her think about her phobia while stimulating (tapping) several meridian points. As the story goes, he spontaneously cured her; she took a swan dive into his backyard pool.

Obviously Callahan was intrigued. His investigation into what had just happened led him to develop Thought Field Therapy. The meridian pathways of energy that we discussed earlier have specific access points along the body. An acupuncturist uses these points to insert needles to promote physical healing. Callahan brilliantly used those same meridian points known in chiropractic and acupuncture to work with the emotional system.

Thought Field Therapy is a collection of algorithms, or tapping sequences on the meridian points. The order of the points is thought to correlate to broad sets of emotion. For instance, there is a Grief Algorithm, a Phobia Algorithm, a Trauma Algorithm, etc. The client moves quickly, tapping through a sequence of meridian points on the body (between 1 and 8 points) while thinking of the problem. So here, the "circuitry" part is the order in which to tap on these meridian points. The "intention" part is always the same: the client tunes in to the presenting problem or traumatic event. So in Thought Field Therapy, the client would think about the phobia (or the anger, or addictive urge, etc.) and follow the therapist through the tapping sequence that best correlates to that emotion category. The assumption here is that when you combine the right tapping sequence with the emotional focus, the original fuel behind the symptom is released from the body and the symptom spontaneously resolves.[18]

In 2008, David Goldstein and John H. Deipold used electroencephalography to measure abnormal brain wave patterns that were observed when a person thought about a trauma when compared with thinking about a neutral (baseline) event.

"Reassessment of brain wave patterns (associated with the traumatic memory) immediately after Thought Field Therapy diagnosis and treatment revealed that the previous abnormal pattern was altered and was no longer statistically abnormal. An 18-month follow-up indicated that the patient continued to be free of all emotional upset regarding the treated trauma. This case study supports the concept that trauma-based negative emotions do have a correlated and measurable abnormal energetic effect. In addition, this study objectively identified an immediate energetic change after thought field therapy in the direction of normalcy and health, which has persisted."[19]

Incidentally, the better-known Emotional Freedom Technique, or E.F.T., made popular by Gary Craig, is the use of Callahan's "Trauma Algorithm" applied to every issue, rather than the use of more specified algorithms based on symptom specificity.[20] Craig reasoned that since the Trauma Algorithm contains all of the points used in all of the algorithms, it would be more efficient to apply that one algorithm in all circumstances and cover every base.

One of the more interesting parts of Callahan's protocol came at the end of each Algorithm. There is a meridian point on the back of the hand, between the little finger and ring-finger bones. It's called the "Triple Warmer" because three of the main meridian pathways end there. Callahan would have the client tap on that point while doing a series of seemingly unrelated things. The client would have to look down to the right, then down to the left, then circle their eyes to the right, then the left. Then the client would have to either count out loud one to five, then five to one, or hum up five notes and then down. All of this had to be performed while still tuning into the emotional distress they were trying to clear. In our training no explanation was given for this series of actions. It was just taught as part of each algorithm and part of what caused change in the client's energy system. Several years later I would realize the logic of what Callahan was trying to do.

## Neuro-Emotional Technique

The main structures of the Splankna Protocol are adapted from Neuro-Emotional Technique.[21] Again, about 20 years ago, the chiropractic community started asking an important question. Chiropractors realized that it isn't optimal for the body to be adjusted and readjusted in the same place, week after week, year after year. So with patients who kept returning with the same spinal misalignment over and over, they started to ask how they could address things differently and have a more permanent effect. When there can be no ergonomic or circumstantial reason found for the subluxation, could there be an emotional component to these repeated misalignments? And if there is an emotional component, do meridians relate to emotions? Sound familiar? It has been assumed for thousands of years in Eastern cultures that there is indeed a relationship between meridians and emotions. In searching for a format to utilize this connection more efficiently, Dr. Scott Walker developed what is now called Neuro-Emotional Technique. He designed a chart of emotions that he found to typically be stored in the 14 main body meridians: anger in liver alarm points, fear in kidneys, and so forth.

The type of "circuitry + intention" that he employed is what I now call "direct access" because he would have the client directly touch the meridian point on the body that was thought to correlate to the presenting emotion. For instance, if the misalignment was being fueled/caused by grief over the loss of a parent, he would have the client touch the Lung or Large Intestine Meridian point, because grief is thought to be "stored" there in the body's energetic system. He would have the client tune in to the grief while touching the point. The theory is that combining that specified touch with the specific intention would facilitate the body to release or resolve the stored emotion and the fuel/cause behind the misalignment would dissolve. The patient's grief was causing his back to go out. Now that the grief was released, his spinal adjustments would hold. Of all the styles of Energy Psychology, this is the one I have personally found to be the most targeted and effective. It tackles the emotions very specifically, like an arrow-shot, as opposed to Thought Field Therapy's more "shotgun" approach.

## E.M.D.R.

I imagine it as a balmy, warm summer in California as Dr. Francine Shapiro enjoyed her afternoon jog. While she ran, she was thinking about a recent situation that was upsetting. She noticed that her eyes started jutting back and forth quickly and her sense of distress melted away. She was surprised by this observation and decided to see if she could do it again. She intentionally thought of something else distressing and started quickly moving her eyes back and forth. Again, her distress seemed to decrease. She, like Callahan, was fascinated by this accidental experience and sought to find out what it meant. She discovered that rapid eye movements correlate to trauma resolution in the brain. It's related to what happens during R.E.M. sleep. When the eyes move quickly back and forth, the movement seems to facilitate trauma processes in the brain to function optimally. The old wives' tale is that we're working out our problems in our sleep; as it turns out, the old wives were on to something.

Dr. Shapiro, a clinical psychologist, developed a treatment protocol that she called *Eye Movement Desensitization and Reprocessing*. She discovered soon after, however, that it wasn't fundamentally the eye movements that were causing the trauma resolution. The real change agent is any kind of bilateral stimulation of the brain hemispheres, meaning anything that stimulates the two sides of the brain back and forth. This can be done, she found, through eye movement, through bilateral (side-to-side) sound, touch, body movement, etc.[22]

E.M.D.R. as it is now called, is different from the other two protocols we've discussed so far because it is non-energetic. It is not utilizing the Meridian System of Energy in the body (at least not directly). But it is a mind-body procedure nonetheless; it is able to access subconscious emotional content and is very useful for trauma resolution. Even though this book is a call to redeem Energy Psychology, and E.M.D.R. is non-energetic, I still include it for two reasons: primarily because it is a part of the protocol I have developed and secondly because it is an effective mind-body tool that often gets lumped into the hands-off/New Age category by Christians. It, too, needs to be redeemed and used to advance the Kingdom.

E.M.D.R. is definitely the best-known and most-respected mind-body treatment protocol in psychology and for good reason. It has impressive research behind it, whereas Energy Psychology protocols tend to have much more sparing and anecdotal research behind them. The main reason for this is that the Meridian System of Energy just doesn't lend itself well to a double-blind study. We don't know enough about it to narrow down all the variables and control issues. And as we've already said, we don't have tools yet to measure it. So for now, effectiveness is still its most convincing proof. Drs. Shapiro, Callahan, Walker, and others have been pioneers in the development of mind-body psychology. Their contributions have been enormous and are yet to be fully realized. I am grateful for their ingenuity and courage.

## Synthesizing

I've given you an explanation of these three styles of mind-body psychology because they are the ones I have drawn from in the development of the Splankna protocol. Here I should tell you the rest of the story of that developmental process from a clinical standpoint.

As I went along, asking God to show me how to redeem these tools and how to clean off the New Age elements, I had two realizations. One of those I have already shared. I noticed that all the different Energy Psychology protocols (and even E.M.D.R.) had one thing in common. They were all doing some form of "circuitry + intention". The other epiphany was about Callahan's elaborate sequence at the triple warmer point. I realized that what he was actually accomplishing through those steps was the very same thing Shapiro had discovered. He was getting at bilateral brain hemisphere stimulation, just by slightly more cumbersome means. And so in my own private practice, I decided to meld the two together. When I use an algorithm, I replace the Triple Warmer 9g sequence with Shapiro's eye movements. This allows a combination of the two that is easier for the client to perform while retaining effectiveness.

One of the challenges that the E.M.D.R. camp faces is that the eye movements are so powerful that they have the potential of re-traumatizing the client. When a client is undergoing the eye movement procedure and tuning into a particular trauma, they often report that they "see it happening" or "see it going by like a train". This re-experiencing can sometimes be emotionally overloading for the client. E.M.D.R. trainers are very conscientious about this potential and carefully train their practitioners to protect the client from re-traumatization. By adding bilateral brain stimulation only at the end of an Algorithm (where Callahan did his 9-G sequence), the potential for re-traumatization is significantly reduced. By the time the body gets to bilateral stimulation, most of the emotional potency has already been neutralized by the Algorithm; the brain balancing is more of a finisher. This discovery and adaptation was the beginning of developing my own Energy Psychology protocol.

To close the clinical definitions section, we need to discuss the tool we use to *access* all of this subconscious trauma storage in the body.

## Muscle Testing

Here is where the question of spiritual boundaries comes most clearly into play. We'll define muscle testing and its theoretical mechanisms here and discuss the apologetics a little later.

As we have established, we are assuming (as does traditional talk-therapy) that previous traumas and the emotions we carry from them are the fuel behind our current psychological symptoms. We have also established that clients, by and large, do not want to have these symptoms. Consciously they already agree with health and wholeness. But within the subconscious, where the traumas are stored, they are still being expressed and falsely "resolved" through symptoms. To put it as simply as possible, the subconscious reacts to these stored, unresolved traumas through symptoms for one of two reasons: either to express the trauma and its need for resolution, like a spotlight to get attention on it, or to use the symptom as a believed coping strategy or resolution for the trauma. Symptoms are typically either the subconscious expression or attempted resolution of an earlier, unresolved trauma.

Unfortunately, we are not usually aware of the correlation between trauma and symptom. When we are aware, that awareness does not typically translate into wholeness. We all have a few areas in our lives where we can identify obvious problems in our behavioral patterns or emotional reactions. We know we are wrong; we may even know where the problem originates, but that knowledge does not solve it. Talking with a therapist about what you already know you need to do is like preaching to the choir. The conscious mind, engaged in traditional therapy, is already on board. What Energy Psychology does is work with the more authentic seat of the problem . . . the subconscious. The subconscious mind has all of one's life experiences catalogued like a hard-drive. This data center is remarkably detailed. For instance, studies in hypnosis have shown that you can recite a song that you only heard once in childhood. So on a subconscious level, there is full awareness of the connections between life traumas and the symptoms that have developed around them. Somehow, to the subconscious mind, those symptoms seem inevitable or necessary, i.e. coping strategies. The subconscious knows when this symptom started and why, even when it is inexplicable to my conscious mind. So how do we *access* this data in the Energy Psychology world? Through muscle testing. Throughout the whole process of trying to seek God and follow His lead on these topics, this was the most difficult part for me to navigate both logically and theologically.

The theory behind muscle testing is that any major muscle in the body that is fairly well isolated will respond to energetic shifts that go off in the body. Further, there seems to be a correlation between muscle strength and congruence. For instance, if my female client holds her arm out strong (activating her deltoid), looks me in the eye, and says something with which she is incongruent, such as, "I am a male," the incongruence of that statement causes a minor, temporary tweak in her energy system. That shows up in a weaker muscle that will not hold under applied pressure. If she says something with which she *is* congruent, it will cause no reaction and her muscle will remain strong.[23]

(I know, hang in there.)

Because the body responds naturally this way to ideas and their congruence, a muscle test can be used as something like a crude "yes/no" tool. It is used in the Splankna protocol (and by others in the field) to help identify the emotions that were felt and stored from a previous trauma and where they resonate or are stored in the body. Once that is identified, the different styles of "circuitry + intention" can be applied to help relieve the intensity of psychological symptoms.

Remember, we are only defining in this section. We will address the theological questions in later chapters. These are three examples of how quantum energy relates to psychology and how the mind-body phenomenon can be navigated. Up until this point, the Christian community has had little to say in response to treatment paradigms like these. We have not asked the difficult questions. We have not delved into their philosophical underpinnings in order to form an intelligent position. It is time we do the work. There is gold to be mined.

In short, the Splankna protocol draws from these three established mind-body protocols and does two things on a clinical level: it removes redundancy and adds prayer. We will discuss Splankna in detail in Chapter 10. There are two main arguments against Christians using tools like these: that they are New Age and that they are witchcraft. In order to evaluate it for spiritual soundness we first need to clarify the accusations. Rather than just slapping a fish symbol on a New Age product, let's take the discussion further.

Now that we've established the basics of energy, of Energy Psychology, let's look at why the Christian community typically avoids this whole field and why I am suggesting that we use it. Of the two main accusations, the most common is the assumption that it should not be used because it's New Age. But I find that when pressed, few Christians can even define what they mean by New Age, much less make a compelling case for abstaining. In this next chapter, let's get clear on what New Age *is* before we land on a verdict.

# CHAPTER 4

# The Basics of New Age

*"Why is it that when we talk to God we're said to be praying,
but when God talks to us we're schizophrenic?"* —Lily Tomlin

One October morning in 1997, I noticed a little ad in the local paper. It was calling for a new director for the regional branch of 1-800-Therapist. I thought that might be fun and a good way to drum up business for my still-miniature private practice. I called the number only to find out that the gentleman who answered had filled the position. We got to talking, though, and discovered we were both believers. We set up a lunch appointment to get to know each other better. He was a few years older than I was and had been in practice for some years. When I explained to him my special interest, he was intrigued and asked me to do a Saturday in-service for his group of 12 Christian counselors.

I had never considered training but was glad to give it a try. I prepared handouts, designed little diagrams—the works. I met the 12 therapists in the group, we prayed together to start the day, and dove in. I wasn't two hours into the day's content when it was painfully obvious that not all of these therapists were believers. Among other things, several of them overtly challenged me on using "combative language" when I was discussing warfare with the enemy and the role it plays in our symptoms. They contended that there is no such thing as warfare or evil because "everything is God's."

I was prepared to be challenged on the New Age front, on the clinical front, and even just the quack front, but I was completely unprepared for this. I had just taken for granted that when the leader of this group said they were all Christians, they were. I hadn't even considered I might be unknowingly handing these powerful tools into the hands of unbelievers. I stood there befuddled in the face of their contention and tried to regroup. As I walked out of the conference room that afternoon, I was really shaken. What if I had just given these tools to people who would use them against God? Was I accountable to God for what they would do? The fact is that to use Energy Psychology tools without getting into New Age philosophy and practice takes careful awareness and scrutiny. I was not about to be responsible for leading people down the wrong path. I vowed that day that I would never train anyone again. It was just too perilous. It's one thing to take a risk for myself, believing I am being called by God. But it's entirely another thing to bring others along.

So what's all the fuss about? Why get so worked up? Because unfortunately, in American culture, alternative psychology (and specifically energy theory) has not risen as a purely therapeutic or even scientific movement. It has risen as a psychophilosophical movement. Implicit underneath *any* theory of change is a theory of humanity, a philosophy of life, and even a theology. Any training program for therapists includes the exploration of spirituality as it relates to emotional health. Both the clients' and the therapists' theology comes unavoidably into play in the therapy room, even if not overtly. The same applies to the recent discoveries in physics and neuroscience that have given rise to energy theories. Maybe unwittingly they have also spawned a theological revolution of sorts.

## The Theology Beneath Change

Until nearly the end of the 17th century theism reigned in our culture. The triune God of the Bible was generally accepted as the benevolent Creator of the universe. His laws were assumed to be moral and applicable to all peoples of all times. The real force of debate was still theological and not yet existential. God's existence, personhood, and creator-hood were not in question. The only issues were things such as how do we *know* God, how do we follow Him, what forms of worship are acceptable? James W. Sire, in *The Universe Next Door*, describes it this way:

> *"Baby John, a child of the seventeenth century . . . was cradled in a cultural consensus that gave a sense of place. The world around was really there —created to be there by God. As God's vice regent, young John sensed being given dominion over the world. He was required to worship God, but God was eminently worthy of worship. He was required to obey God, but then obedience to God was true freedom since that was what people were made for."*

Obviously, this is no longer an accurate description of our society. Now Christians truly are foreigners and aliens in this world. Even American culture, founded on faith, now bears only remnants of Christianity. When my parents were growing up, the culture around them accepted, for the most part, the basic moral standard prescribed by Christianity. The gap was small between Christianity and culture. But that congruence has swiftly decayed in the last several decades. No longer can believers relax in comfortable social agreement and support of their position. Now for the Body of Christ, daily interaction with society reveals a sharp contrast in paradigm and we have learned to be wary of whatever consensus promotes—and rightly so. Increasingly, popular culture will contradict the truth. It is not only rational but necessary for the contemporary Christian to be skeptical and discerning of what current culture endorses. The emergence of alternative psychology has coincided with and contributed to a significant shift toward humanism in our cultural theological foundation. It must be evaluated with that in mind.

Kevin McFarland of Manna International tells a story of observing a young boy in an airport in Port-au-Prince, Haiti. The boy was watching through the window as people boarded their planes and flew off into the sunset. The odd thing was that each time a plane would fly off, the boy would break into hysterical laughter. McFarland watched this process for some time before his curiosity overtook him. He approached the boy and asked why he was laughing at the planes. The boy looked up and said, "If those people only knew how tiny they were going to be in just a few minutes, they would never get on those planes!" Worldview affects everything.

Because of its historical origins, alternative psychology is understood and described, for the most part, through an Eastern philosophical worldview. So in order for us to rationally discuss the separation of the physiopsychological mechanisms in alternative psychology from its philosophical underpinnings, we need to examine what those underpinnings are.

## Early Origins of Mind-Body Work

*"A lie can travel half way around the world
while the truth is putting on its shoes." —Mark Twain*

Eastern scholars are primarily credited with the early discoveries of the connection between the mind and body and its possible treatments. Subsequently, the majority of known information on the mind-body connection has been filtered through the Eastern philosophical lens. Eastern thought approaches healing, physical and emotional, from a systemic perspective—assuming that mind, body, and emotion are inexplicably intertwined and that balance among these parts is synonymous with health. Illness and emotional pain, seasons and sorrows are all assumed to be interdependent.

An Eastern practitioner of health might prescribe an herbal treatment for the feet to treat panic disorder. He would conceptualize the whole person (as well as the environment/universe) as a unified whole, so the best treatment for the mind might be through the foot. Subsequently, current alternative psychology, because of being rooted in Eastern thought, tends to look at change systemically. The general assumption is that *balance* is the goal for health, whether physical or emotional. For instance, a "systemic balance" theory of change will look for all imbalances in the person's whole system (body, mind, emotion, spirit, etc.) and seek to correct those imbalances through the most effective means available.

The assumption of systemic interconnection is not usually congruent with Western medical or psychological thought. Western thought assumes that symptoms like arthritis and mania are irrelevant to one another— unrelated. The body and the mind are assumed to operate independently of one another—two self-contained organisms. A Western practitioner would find it ridiculous to treat a mental disorder through the foot or heart disease through forgiveness. But a biblical worldview *does* support the interconnectedness between the whole system.

A systemic perspective, however, is not the only thing that characterizes the Eastern worldview. If it were, there would probably be no barrier between the Christian worldview and that of alternative psychology. But as we've established, alternative psychology has come with more than Eastern holism. Over the centuries, Eastern religious culture has undergone transformation just as American culture has, integrating many schools of thought, including Hinduism, Buddhism, Pantheism, Universalism, Taoism, and others. Unavoidably, early Eastern practitioners of medicine and psychology described their findings about the mind-body connection in terms consistent with their religious beliefs; in terms that Western culture now refers to as "New Age". There are several excellent books currently in print that cover the New Age movement from a Christian perspective, such as Douglas Groothuis' *Unmasking the New Age* (InterVarsity, 1986) and the previously mentioned *The Universe Next Door* by James W. Sire (InterVarsity, 1997). These are excellent resources for a more exhaustive description of New Age, its history, and its components.

In order to take an intelligent crack at sifting out the New Age elements here, we should first get clear on the basics of the New Age mindset. The term "New Age" is used very broadly for a wide array of contemporary and ancient beliefs and practices. It's about as broad a term as "religion". But there are a few fundamentals upon which most New Age proponents would agree. Here we are going to state those briefly to get a reference for discussion.

## Monism/Pantheism

*"Separation is a dream from which we need to awaken . . .*
*joining with each other and undoing the separation*
*which gave rise to the dream." —A Course in Miracles*

From the furthest cosmos to the smallest subatomic particle, New Age declares that all is "one". Formally this is called *Monism* (from *mono* meaning one). It is the belief that there is no separateness in the universe— not only between people but between everything that exists. All things are thought to be part of one whole energy or consciousness (spirit). The rock, the wind, a person, a star all may appear separate but are really not merely interrelated or interdependent but totally "one". Our experience of separateness is mere illusion and is created and supported by our collective agreement with it. One of the main tasks of enlightenment is to come to the realization and acceptance of this oneness and allow all fantasies of separateness to disappear. God is seen as the universal animating principle, without personhood. Neale Donald Walch claims in his book *Conversations With God* to quote "God" in saying:

> *"You are always a part of God, because you are never apart from God. This is the truth of your being. We are Whole. So now you know the whole truth . . . So go ahead! Mix what you call the profane and the profound—so that you can see that there is no difference, and experience All as One . . . I Am What I Am: All That Is."*

Recently I spent a few hours on the phone with a young woman who reported having several "transcendent experiences". I asked her if there is a God inside that reality. She replied, "Well, God is everything, and I am a part of everything. There's no difference." From a New Age perspective, the goal is for one to become aware of and surrendered to this "oneness". The Buddhists call this epiphany nirvana, Hindus call it satchitananada, and Zen calls it satori—the final recognition is that you do not actually exist. There is no you, and there is no one else. All is one.

> "All is interrelated, interdependent, and interpenetrating. Ultimately there is no difference between God, a person, a carrot or a rock. They are all part of one continuous reality that has no boundaries, no ultimate division. Any perceived differences between separate entities – between Joe and Judy or between Joe and a tree or between God and Judy — are only apparent and not real."[24]

71

J. Keel says it this way in his book *The Eighth Tower*:

> *"The standard definition of God, 'God is light,' is just a simple way of saying that God is energy. Electromagnetic energy. He is not a 'He', but an 'It;' a field of energy that permeates the entire universe and, perhaps, feeds off the energy generated by its component parts."*[25]

This is a tempting concept. It sounds very sophisticated, so respectful and centered. It sounds like it honors all things and trivializes nothing. Its proponents make the consciousness of separateness seem so small and uninspired. I have heard confused Christian clients who think this "oneness" is a biblical postulate. I've heard them argue that it's what Paul is trying to say in Romans 11:36, when he explains that *from him and through him and to him are all things*. But is it really?

Pantheism is very similar and also commonly underlying New Age practices. *Pantheism* (Greek: πάν (pan) = all and θεός (theos) = God, literally "God is all" -ism) is the view that everything is part of an all-encompassing eminent God and that the Universe (Nature) and God are equivalent. Pantheism promotes the idea that God is better understood as an abstract principle representing natural law, existence, and the Universe (the sum total of all that was, is, and shall be), rather than as an anthropomorphic (personal) entity.

Simply put, pantheism asserts that *nature is god*; that the observable universe and god are identical. God is thought to be the generic life force that permeates all things. There is no real matter, for all things are manifestations of "spirit". Disney gave us a spectacular illustration of pantheism in *Pocahontas*. The young Indian maiden is depicted as the wiser, enlightened Native American contrasted with the savage, Western antagonist who has no respect for nature or mankind. She sings,

*"You think you own whatever land you land on*
*The Earth is just a dead thing you can claim*
*But I know every rock and tree and creature*
*Has a life, has a spirit, has a name . . .*
*Have you ever heard the wolf cry to the blue corn moon?*
*Or asked the grinning bobcat why he grinned?*
*Can you sing with all the voices of the mountains?*
*Can you paint with all the colors of the wind?*
*The rainstorm and the river are my brothers*
*The heron and the otter are my friends*
*And we are all connected to each other*
*In a circle, in a hoop that never ends . . . ."*

—*Colors of the Wind*

Nature itself is portrayed as the living, pulsing, perfect center of innate life and wisdom. The film promises that if we only connect, listen, and learn, nature will be our god and teach us all truth. You could know what the squirrel and the bald eagle know if you'd only be quiet and listen. They know far more than you do. It's a seemingly self-denying, paradoxical piety.

## Evil Does Not Exist

*"Good and evil have no absolute reality."*
—*Swami Adbhutananda*

Now obviously, if all is "one," then there cannot be any evil in the biblical sense (or any other sense, for that matter). Nothing can really be good either. Neutrality is the only logical option, although New Age opts for the "all is good position" because it feels so much better. But in order for something to be good or evil, there would have to be some kind of distinction between things. And if all is "one", there is no distinction, no value judgment. In fact, judgment itself is sacrilege to the New Age advocate. One is considered unenlightened—nearly prehistoric—when attempting to discern or judge any thing or any thought, since discernment implies separateness. Ironically, since there actually is such a thing as good and evil, the New Age attempt to devalue all things in the name of unity ends up in practical naiveté. Since we are incapable with any integrity to really convince ourselves that all is neutral, the New Ager, in practicality ends up calling all "good", even "divine".

Part and parcel with the absence of evil is the absence of death. If we're going to fashion reality however we'd like it to be, then let's go all the way. Reincarnation replaces the heaven and hell of antiquity. We go on and on through endless rehearsals of life in order to become more and more enlightened. Not more and more good, mind you, since all is one anyway, but more and more aware of that fact of oneness until we can melt into it and cease to exist. This is "nirvana". It is amazing how American culture has sugarcoated these Eastern concepts until they are beyond recognition.

## Inner Divinity

*"Every person is a God in embryo. Its only desire*
*is to be born." —Deepak Chopra*

In his book on Reflexology, D. Berkson explains, "We all possess healing powers of the universe within us, and we all have the right and ability to call upon the healing power of god, nature, or whatever we feel comfortable calling it."[26] It is a short jump from Monism, Pantheism, and the absence of evil to the crowning New Age belief that all is "god". Like we've said, since we cannot authentically convince ourselves into neutrality (and it isn't nearly as fun), let's default to universal divinity. The rock is god, the computer on my lap is god, and of course, and most importantly, I am god. Just waiting to be unleashed from within me is perfect knowledge, power, wisdom, and awareness. My biggest challenge is merely accepting it, allowing it. It's the New Age Gospel. Chakra work (which focuses on theoretical energy axes along the body's midline) aims at balancing and opening up the body's energy centers in order to facilitate the upward movement of the Kundalini Serpent through the body. For the Hindus, the snake Kundalini symbolizes the hidden supernatural energy slumbering in every man.[27]

It sounds preposterous, of course, when put so blatantly. But let's be honest, when presented *subtly* is there anything more beguiling? Could any philosophical suggestion be more enticing? If I only learn to tap into it, everything divine is within me, waiting to be manifested.

I do believe that deep within the heart of every human being there is an innate awareness—an awareness both of our *imago dei* and of our inherent fallenness. If one did not have a biblical world- and self-view, I can see how easy it would be to go with the former. But in essence, it's just the original lie in new clothing. It's like we're eavesdropping on an old conversation with that same snake.

## Truth Confusion

*"Say not, 'I have found the truth,' but rather,*
*'I have found a truth.'" —Kahlil Gibran*

Sit down at Starbucks with the average 24-year-old New Age sage and you'll notice a delicate and interesting contradiction. In the same conversation he will explain that there is no "absolute truth", but in the next breath he will contend that everything is true. It's remarkable really how a New Age philosopher will actually make *both* points if argued with long enough. He will tell you, on the one hand, how your truth, my truth, it's all leading down the same road—all really saying the same thing . . . all true. And yet he will contend vigorously that there is no such thing as "absolute" truth because of the very same argument . . . yours is no better than mine and your archaic "truth" is infringing on my divinity. Ultimately, he will tell you, the source of all truth and knowledge is *within* each person (even though he just told you there wasn't any). It's just waiting to be tapped; it is above and beyond our finite, conscious ability to grasp it. He will explain to you that all religions are really different versions of one reality and that all the "enlightened ones" of all religions throughout history had caught on to this. They were all different manifestations of "spirit" in someone who figured out the secret of the universe. This also sounds so sociologically respectful. The exclusivity claim of Christianity is so stark, that set against this cultural backdrop of inclusivity it easily seems backward and arrogant.

A local church here in Colorado embodies the beliefs we've described so far. They describe their creed as follows:

1.  We recognize the divinity in all living beings.

2.  We validate and support spiritual growth in ourselves and others.

3.  We foster an understanding and acceptance of all faith traditions.

4.  We commit to participating in our world as good citizens of our local community and the global village.

5.  We support spiritual freedom and new paradigms to foster love, light, and harmony in the universe. Our church community is growing steadily, we welcome the presence of children, and we have no specific dogma or belief system that

must be adhered to. We are a new church for the 21st century and would be pleased to welcome you to our services and activities.

This was her first session. She had come for advice on dating. She was a professed Christian, so I reiterated what we understand to be God's design for romance and marriage—generally that men are designed to initiate and women are designed to respond. (She tended to be the pursuer in her romantic life.) God's designs in the masculine and feminine heart allow them to fit together like puzzle pieces. His pursuer/responder pattern creates a positive vicious cycle and desire grows mutually. She responded curtly, "I'm glad for you that traditional gender roles *happen* to work for you and your husband. As for me, I'm finding my own truth as I go." I guess anybody's *truth* will do.

## We Create Reality

*"Reality is merely an illusion, albeit a very persistent one."*
—*Albert Einstein*

I saw an intriguing advertisement on my Yahoo mail page a few years ago. You've probably seen it, too. It was just a simple black box with white lettering inside that said "Do you want to know the Secret?" and it prompted me to go to *www.TheSecret.tv*. Due to the deluge of constant Internet gimmicks, I ignored it. But I continued to hear about it for months after that. When clients began asking me if I'd seen the documentary version, I figured I'd better see what all the commotion was about.

*The Secret* is a compilation of interviews with various "enlightened" individuals that explains what they claim has been known by every wise and successful person throughout history. They claim with great drama that it has been kept a secret so that the power and money it provides could be kept among the elite. They say that they are now, for no other reason than altruistic generosity, sharing it with you. The big "secret", they say, is that your intention creates reality. You are the author of your entire life and every event within it.

Regardless of the hype, this message is not new. It's been used to make millions by the self-help crowd for decades. And of course ultimately it's *still* capitalizing on the same lie from the Garden . . . "you are god." The documentary goes through countless examples and testimonies from known and obscure contributors showing how everything you think manifests in some form of reality or event. They assure you that you can "manifest" anything you want. "Do you want wealth?" they ask. "Do you want love in your life, or perfect health?" Anything you want, you can manifest by controlling your thoughts. You can think anything into existence.

They use simple, daily examples like driving to work. They explain how if you're thinking throughout your drive, "I'm going to be late! I'm going to be late!" . . . then you will be. But if you are driving the whole time thinking, "I'm going to make it! I'm going to make it!" . . . then you will! They assert that you have "created" every aspect of your life and that you simply need to become aware of it and do a better job of it. Supposedly every rich and powerful person throughout history got that way by employing this "secret" and creating their own realities. You can do the same, they say.

*The Secret* is a formal example of a long-held common theme in New Age thinking. This idea runs through all the others and unifies them. As with the other tenets of New Age philosophy, it is, believe it or not, mostly true with a critically evil twist. But we'll get to that later. Along with the doctrine of inner divinity, it is the limitless potential here that is so tempting. If I have created everything I've ever experienced, then potentially I can harness my innate power and create a *perfect* life. Who wouldn't want to really be in control of their life?

## Cosmic Evolutionary Optimism

*"Our civilization is now in the transition stage between the age of warring empires and a new age of world unity and peace."*
*—John Boyd Orr*

So if all things are one, we are all god, and we create reality, then why is the human race such a mess? New Age cries, "Because we haven't *'gotten it'* yet!" Eventually we'll get it. At some point soon we'll figure it out, become enlightened as a species, and finally hit a critical mass in development. This will lead to the next evolutionary leap into divinity; we stand now at its precipice. New Age preaches that we have the capacity individually and corporately to become fully divine and that we will eventually do this on our own power. Very soon, the human race will catapult itself into godhood; consciousness, as we now know it, will cease. A well-known futurist, Barbara Marx Hubbard, admonishes us to lay aside "crisis futurism" and adopt "evolutionary futurism" which maintains, "we may even expect a new suprahuman species which will be 'as superior to present day humanity as we are to the apes.'"[28] We will be able to take the reins of evolution in hand and reconstruct the future of the human race.

Jesus was an example of someone who caught on to this ahead of His time, they say. He was not inherently different than any of us. He just understood His connection with "spirit" and His inner divinity in a way that we only strive toward. All the other great masters—Buddha, Confucius, Mohammed, etc.—are on the same plane with Him. And we could all attain their level of spiritual advancement with enough understanding and effort. Meditation techniques and other styles of consciousness alteration are used in New Age practices to help one arrive at this awareness of inner divinity, enlightenment, and oneness. Even Yoga, recently embraced by many in the Christian community, shares in its original intention this same goal.

New Age rhetoric claims that humanity's central problem is that we are *unaware* of our godhood. If we could just come into the cosmic realization that we are simply part of the "one", and so is God, and therefore we *are* God, all would be righted. If we only fully understood that, we could be or do or become or experience anything we could dream up. The New Age practitioner encourages this shift in consciousness—from simple one-dimensional, limited humanness to a conscious acknowledgement of one's inherent godhood—as the quintessential prerequisite to becoming whole. Ultimate self-actualization cannot occur while a person is limited to humanity and the illusion of separateness. And the more individuals (as if individuality could exist) attain this enlightenment, eventually the human race will reach divinity as a whole.

Tied to this optimistic expectation is a belief that the *road* to perfection/divinity is within us. We've mentioned how remarkable both the awareness level and the data collection processes are in the subconscious. New Age philosophy makes the jump from this observation to the assumption that the subconscious is our center of all knowledge and wisdom—that subconsciously we already know everything about the universe and one another. The task is to tap into it as well as to the avatars of the past, including Jesus. The subconscious is elevated far above its place into divinity as well. New Age has morphed Carl Jung's concept of the collective subconscious into the belief that at the subconscious level, every individual knows everything about everyone—past, present, and future.

## Muscle Testing

Following right along with the assumption that the subconscious contains all wisdom as well as data, New Age elevates muscle testing as well.

As an aside here, it needs to be said that muscle testing was clearly not God's original design. Obviously we were not originally intended to need to push on each other's arms to deal with our hearts. I think it is something like a hearing aid for later days. We live in a bizarre little time-frame within the big story. The kind of sensory overload that we experience as normal is absurd and unprecedented in all of human history. We sit in a supposedly quiet room and are bombarded with radio waves and electro-magnetic frequencies. We live under power lines and sleep next to our cell phones. No other humans since Adam have had to tolerate this kind of sensory stimulation. They couldn't even conceive of it. We don't even realize it because we're fish in water. We can no longer hear our own hearts like we used to. If my entire day consisted of sitting on the hillside—looking after the sheep in the distance and watching the blades of grass bend in the breeze—I could write psalms, too. I believe that muscle testing is a concession for our predicament. Now, back to our train of thought.

Since the subconscious is thought to have all the desired information and muscle testing is thought to be able to access it, without any consideration for the weakness and limitations of that tool, muscle testing is hailed by some as the genie's instrument of all knowledge. A few years ago, a believing couple that work in the holistic health field recommended a book to me. They were big fans. The book was called *Power vs. Force.* Here's an excerpt from the back cover copy:

> *"Imagine . . . what if you had access to a simple yes-or-no answer to any question you wished to ask?*
> *A demonstrably true answer.*

*Any question . . .*
*Think about it."*

Yes, let's do. Let's think about that and notice how obviously absurd it is. But it sums up the misuse and perversion of muscle testing by the New Age community. And once again, how enticing? Who wouldn't want to be able to have the answer to anything? Haven't we been looking for all knowledge from the beginning? We were shown the "tree of the knowledge of good and evil"; it seemed irresistible. The New Bible Dictionary discusses this issue:

"Many views of the meaning of 'the knowledge of good and evil' in this context have been put forward. One of the most common would see it as the knowledge of right and wrong, but it is difficult to suppose that Adam did not already possess this, and that, if he did not, he was forbidden to acquire it. Others would connect it with the worldly knowledge that comes to man with maturity, and which can be put to either a good or bad use. Another view would take the expression 'good and evil' as an example of a figure of speech whereby an antonymic pair signifies totality, meaning therefore 'everything' and in the context universal knowledge. Against this is the fact that Adam, having eaten of the tree, did not gain universal knowledge. Yet another view would see this as a quite ordinary tree, which was selected by God to provide an ethical test for the man, who 'would acquire an experiential knowledge of good or evil according as he was steadfast in obedience or fell away into disobedience'".[29]

Whatever the specific meaning, one thing is clear from the Genesis account: man was enticed by special knowledge and power and the promise of "being like God".

We still are.

# CHAPTER 5

# Our Response to New Age

*What do you get when you cross a Zen Buddhist with a Wiccan?*
*Someone who worships the tree that is not there.*

Ａs a Christian community we need to be as clear as possible about what's wrong with these New Age beliefs. Commonly we are not. We are much more confused than convicted.

One night at the end of a session, a believing client of mine said excitedly, "Oh, I saw this great movie. You have to go see it. It's about what you do!" "I highly doubt that," I thought to myself. It was called, *"What the Bleep Do We Know?"* She couldn't really explain it but said it was quite the film phenomenon and that I should check it out, so my husband Jon and I got tickets to the 9 p.m. showing.

As we stood in a surprisingly long line to get into the theatre, everyone around us was buzzing. People were all talking about the movie and the things they had heard. No one seemed very sure what it was we were about to see, but there was unusual anticipation, especially for a documentary. As the lights dimmed, we were greeted by experts of different kinds—physicists, philosophers, professors, etc., in what appeared to be a documentary on quantum physics. The main premise of the movie is that quantum physics proves that we are all made up of energy—that all the universe is one, that we are the creators of reality, and that we design our own lives through our thoughts, intentions, and expectations. The film explained through many convincing special effects that on the quantum level everything is fluid, dynamic, and controlled by thought. So things only exist if I think they do. They even go so far in this movie as to say that an object doesn't exist unless I think it does or until I look at it. They propose that *everything* that happens in our lives is scripted by our subconscious expectations and desires. When the lights came back up, I wanted to jump up onto the stage and preach to the Athenians.

The main scientific problem with this film is that it applies the rules of quantum physics to the macro world—an impossibility. In the field of science they understand that the laws of quantum physics (subatomic particles and their behavior) are extremely reliable and that the laws of Newtonian or macrophysics (all the big stuff we live with) are also extremely reliable. But the fascinating thing is that these two thoroughly "true" sets of laws stand in apparent contradiction to one another. So far, science cannot explain how both of these sets of laws can be true at the same time. Subsequently they have been looking for what they call the "unification theory" for decades—the Holy Grail of physics. This film ignores that inconsistency and applies the laws of quantum physics to the macro level.

Truthfully, there are so *many* problems with this movie that it would take its own whole book to really respond thoroughly. I bring it up because it's a great example of the typical way that the Christian community misses the mark in discernment. My client was an honest, wholehearted believer. She knew the Word. And yet she was unable to spot the lies streaming through this movie. We cannot afford to be naïve. We are the hands and feet of Christ, but we are also His voice. If you are apologetically inclined at all, I highly recommend you familiarize yourself with this film. It is a slick, influential representation of the spirit of the age. Believers should be equipped to respond intelligently to its propositions.

## Monism/Pantheism

The rise of New Age physics can be understood as an overreaction to the reductionism of classical physics. Classical physics was analytical and atomistic. It defined everything in terms of the behavior of its smallest components and failed to take account of integrated systems. But New Age physicists fall off the horse on the opposite side. Whereas classical physics exaggerates the role of parts, [New Age] exaggerate wholes.[30] I am amazed at the power of this one little concept. All is one. At first glance it almost seems insignificant, even semantic. What's the big deal? What's the great harm in seeing all as "one"? Doesn't God say that all things exist in Him and through Him and for Him? Let's look at the remarkable impact of this idea.

If you take a moment to ponder "oneness" and particularly the concepts it leads to, you will find that it undercuts literally every foundation of Christian thought. If all is one, what happens to Lordship? There cannot be Lord and servant or even creator and creature if all is one. What about obedience? By definition one cannot obey another, whether god or man, if all is one. How can I cry out to the Lord in times of need and distress if He has no personhood—if He is just an extension of myself?

Remarkably, even love itself is shattered by oneness. Love denotes an object. Oneness rules out the existence of an object. In a universe of one, love is irrational. Even traditional psychology asserts that one of the fundamental undercurrents of human existence is the dynamic tension between a person's need to be connected and his need to be separate. If all is "one", neither can exist. The idea of relationship *itself* is obsolete. No one could ever write about this truth because it would require the writer to *comment* on what he believes to be the empirical basis for his opinion. Separateness is implicit in comment. It is internally inconsistent. This seemingly benign, inconsistent concept of universal oneness is actually crucially destructive. As believers we must not take it lightly. We must not allow ourselves to be seduced by its feigned respect for all that is. Scripture is more than clear about this.

Monism can be trumped in one word . . . *holy*. We usually think of holiness in terms of purity, righteousness, goodness, etc., but its literal Greek and Hebrew translation is "separated".[31] God is separate from His creation. He is ontologically distinct. He is profoundly *other*. He makes this vividly clear throughout the Word. God tells us plainly that His ways and thoughts are not ours. *God is in heaven and you are on earth* states Ecclesiastes 5:2. The very word *"Emmanuel"*, meaning *"God with us"*, implies that He previously was not. *"Emmanuel"* connotes that it was *remarkable* for God to take human form and live among us, not that this was the normal state of affairs.

We are shown countless times throughout Scripture that the universe does contain not only separateness but hierarchy as well. *Hierarchy* can be understood as a structured, multi-level authority system. All things spiritual are built on authority. In Matthew 8, Jesus is confronted by a Centurion (Roman guard) who asks him to *"say the word"* for his servant to be healed. The Centurion goes on to explain this simple request. He equates his own hierarchical position with that of Jesus. He says that because he has men under him to whom he gives commands, and that they follow, he understands that Jesus, possessing far greater authority than he does, needs only to *say the word*. Jesus is astonished by this man and exclaims that he has *"never seen such faith in all of Israel!"*

By this reaction Jesus clearly validates that He is indeed in hierarchical authority over all of heaven and earth, all things material and spiritual. But

86

New Age teaching denies all forms of hierarchy and authority by equalizing all of existence. By definition, there cannot be hierarchy if God and man are one, because hierarchy requires *difference* of status and authority. The unavoidable outgrowth of this lie is that it renders God's *Lordship* totally void. It is not possible to honor God without acknowledging His Lordship. If all is one and all are god, then there is no worship, no submission, no repentance of sin, no surrender or even trust. All of these things can only be ascribed to a being intrinsically *above* me. None of these ideas makes sense otherwise. Again, by definition, I cannot *worship* my equal; God is to be worshiped. This aspect of New Age thinking is irreconcilable with the Word of God. There is no way around it.

On the other hand, the oneness idea is a brilliant scheme of the deceiver. The New Age worldview gives its followers all the wonder and none of the difficulty. We can be all powerful, all beautiful, and all knowing without ever stepping one foot toward surrender. I believe the most terrifying thing a human being can face is surrender to the grace of God. It is so all-encompassing, so completely out of our control, that it requires the deepest risk a human can take. David Wilcox sings, "Do I dare believe and let love lead my life? Could I not believe and leave that love behind? But love remains . . . to break the chains . . . of those who would dare to trust it."[32] To allow oneself to embrace grace, total unconditional redemption, in the face of the deep depravity we can all sense (if we are honest with ourselves at all), is a feat higher than any daredevil has dreamed. We are just too familiar with betrayal, with trusting hopefully, only to find that others cannot truly bear our darkness gracefully. How can God bear it? Within the New Age paradigm, I never have to even *consider* surrender or trust. So I can spend my lifetime comfortably chasing the theological carrot of eventual god-hood without ever risking submission. Neil Anderson states it pointedly in *The Biblical Guide to Alternative Medicine*: "fallen humanity tries to depersonalize God, because an impersonal god doesn't have to be served."[33]

It is ironic that Christianity is often seen as philosophically cowardly when the exact opposite is true. It is *New Age* that skirts the soul's authentic test. Christianity confronts it head on, but New Age whispers the serpent's tale . . .

> *"There is no surrender needed."*

> *"The only difference between God and yourself is your decision to grasp what is His."*

> *"Reach out, no strings attached."*

> *"You will surely not die."*

But the Scriptures couldn't be clearer on this. *"Choose for yourselves this day whom you will serve!"* (Josh. 24:15). We read in Isaiah that the Lord *sits enthroned above the circle of the earth, and its people are like grasshoppers* (Isa. 40:22). *The Lord is in his holy temple; the Lord is on his heavenly throne. He observes the sons of men; his eyes examine them* (Ps. 11:4) *Let them praise the name of the Lord, for his name alone is exalted; his splendor is above the earth and the heavens* (Ps. 148:13). It sounds so elementary to make this argument, but God cannot be portrayed as being *in* His temple, *on* His throne, "observing", or *above* if all is one. All these descriptions denote separateness. The canon is full of these types of references.

Scripture is unambiguous about this. God is hierarchically above us. Acts 17:24-26 tells us:

> *"The God who made the world and everything in it is the Lord of heaven and earth and does not live in temples built by hands. And he is not served by human hands as if he needed anything, because he himself gives all men life and breath and*

*everything else. From one man he made every nation of men, that they should inhabit the whole earth; and he determined the times set for them and the exact places where they should live."*

The entire Christian worldview implies and necessitates both separateness and hierarchy. Oneness destroys it. Without separateness and hierarchy, every framework we are given in Scripture and every experience we have of relating to a Holy God is not only undermined, it is annihilated. God is separate from us and hierarchically above us.

In Romans 11 we hear of *the depth of the riches of the wisdom and knowledge of God*! How unsearchable his judgments, and his paths beyond tracing out! Isaiah tells us that His thoughts are not our thoughts and His ways are not ours. *For who has understood the mind of the Lord, or instructed him as his counselor?* (Isa. 40:13). If separateness and hierarchy do exist in the universe, then all of those basic structures within which we live every day are restored to their place. Even in common daily interaction, the New Ager is self-contradictory. It is nearly impossible to structure a single day upholding the concept of oneness if one is intellectually honest about its implications.

Although it is obviously beyond the scope of this book to explore thoroughly, New Age also extends Monism directly into religion.

## All Religions Are One

Who hasn't heard the old fable of the blind men and the elephant?

*It was six men of Indostan*
*To learning much inclined,*
*Who went to see the Elephant*

*(Though all of them were blind)*
*That each by observation*
*Might satisfy his mind.*

*The First approach'd the Elephant,*
*And happening to fall*
*Against his broad and sturdy side,*
*At once began to bawl:*
*"God bless me! But the Elephant*
*Is very like a wall!"*

*The Second, feeling of the tusk,*
*Cried, "Ho! What have we here*
*So very round and smooth and sharp?*
*To me 'tis mighty clear*
*This wonder of an Elephant*
*Is very like a spear!"*

*The Third approached the animal,*
*And happening to take*
*The squirming trunk within his hands,*
*Thus boldly up and spake:*
*"I see," quoth he, "the Elephant*
*Is very like a snake!"*

*The Fourth reached out his eager hand,*
*And felt about the knee.*
*"What most this wondrous beast is like*
*Is mighty plain," quoth he,*
*"Tis clear enough the Elephant*
*Is very like a tree!"*

*The Fifth, who chanced to touch the ear,*
*Said: "E'en the blindest man*
*Can tell what this resembles most;*

*Deny the fact who can,*
*This marvel of an Elephant*
*Is very like a fan!"*

*The Sixth no sooner had begun*
*About the beast to grope,*
*Then, seizing on the swining tail*
*That fell within his scope,*
*"I see," quoth he, "the Elephant*
*Is very like a rope!"*

*And so these men of Indostan*
*Disputed loud and long,*
*Each in his own opinion*
*Exceeding stiff and strong,*
*Though each was partly in the right*
*And all were in the wrong!*
*Moral.*

*So oft in theologic wars,*
*The disputant, I ween,*
*Rail on in utter ignorance*
*Of what each other mean,*
*And prate about an Elephant*
*Not one of them has seen!*

*—John Godfrey Saxe, 1873*

The assertion that "all *religions* are one" (Universalism) is the epitome of current political correctness. The sophisticated rally to the cry that "your god and my god are equally acceptable and are really the same". Kahlil Gibran, a well-published voice of New Age thought, supposedly quotes God in "The Voice of the Poet" as saying, "I love you when you bow in your mosque, kneel in your temple, pray in your church. For you and I are sons of one religion, and it is the Spirit." Anyone who does not "realize" this is seen as small-minded and antiquated. They ignorantly hold to their little piece of the Elephant. Yet even a cursory investigation into the major world religions proves they cannot possibly be reconciled. Islam dogmatically claims that it contains the only true revelation of God, which thoroughly contradicts Christianity's claim of exclusive revelation. Buddhism claims that all is *nothing*–that we are only "a collection of states", while Hinduism claims the aforementioned philosophy that "all is one" and that all we see around us is an illusion.[34] There is clear contradiction here before we even *begin* to examine the claims of Christ. We cannot be nothing *and* everything, individual *and* one.

## Evil Does Not Exist/Inner Divinity

If the New Ager does attempt to hold to the oneness doctrine, then the most logical conclusion is that all is neutral, or valueless. But this is far too depressing. So they opt for the belief that everything is good, even divine. It's much more fun for the ego. But of course we don't have to go far in Scripture to contradict this one. *For all have sinned, and fall short of the glory of God* will do it (Rom. 3:23). And there are numerous other biblical citations to concur. Just before the flood, in Noah's time, *the Lord saw how great man's wickedness on the earth had become, and that every inclination of the thoughts of his heart was only evil all the time* (Gen. 6:5). That tree in the Garden contained the *"knowledge of good and evil"*; the entire purpose for the Cross was to redeem mankind from sin. There are actually 477 references to evil in the canon. Hypocritically, while our culture so embraces New Age thought, one still hears the average unbeliever with the same contention against God: that there couldn't be a loving God because there's so much evil in the world.

As for our supposed inherent divinity, Ezekiel 28:2 tells us that, *"Son of man, say to the ruler of Tyre, 'This is what the Sovereign Lord says:*

*In the pride of your heart you say, 'I am a god;*
*I sit on the throne of a god*
*In the heart of the seas.'*
*But you are a man and not a god,*
*Though you think you are as wise as a god."*

## Cosmic Evolutionary Optimism

*"Society has always seemed to demand a little more from*
*human beings than it will get in practice."*[35] —*George Orwell*

Dr. Groothuis coined the term *cosmic evolutionary optimism* to describe the great New Age expectation. It stands to reason that if we have the full potential for divinity within us, just waiting to be mined, and we continue to advance as a human race in knowledge and enlightenment (which New Agers believe we are, and always have), then eventually we will arrive at manifest godhood. Even some Christian circles have taken on a form of this lie. "Faith" teaching, in extreme, promotes the doctrine that the believers who merely "claim" their position in Christ, their authority as His co-heir, and their right to trample the enemy, should expect no trauma, no illness, no want (material or otherwise), and no limitations of spiritual power. However, the Word clearly states that *"in this world you will have trouble"* (John 16:33). Paul bemoans his frustrating battle with his fallen *flesh* in Romans 7:24. Even in Christ, fallenness remains and godhood is *not* the believer's goal. The frighteningly popular recent series *Conversations with God* by Neale Walsch states that God told him " . . . you could move to godhood this instant if you chose to."[36]

*"One day a group of eminent scientists got together and*
*decided that mankind had come a long way and no longer*

*needed God. So they picked one scientist to go and tell Him that they were done with Him. The scientist walked up to God and said, 'God, we've decided that we no longer need you. We're to the point that we can clone people and do many miraculous things, so why don't you just retire?' God listened very patiently to the man and then said, 'Very well, but first, how about this: Let's have a Man-making contest.' The scientist replied, 'Okay, great!' But God added, 'Now, we're going to do this just like I did back in the old days with Adam.' The scientist said, 'Sure, no problem' and bent down and grabbed himself a handful of dirt. God looked at him and said, 'No, no, you go get your own dirt!'" —Author Unknown*

Not only are we not gods now, we never will be. God gives us no indication that we are capable on our own of *ever* attaining equality with Him. Referring to the wisdom of God, David the psalmist writes simply, *Such knowledge is too wonderful for me, too lofty for me to attain* (Ps. 139:6). The New Testament explains that our righteousness is like filthy rags before the Lord (Isa. 64:6).

The climax of mankind's evolution is destruction by fire and the necessity by God to make all things new. The earth itself testifies to this. The universe is not evolving. It is decaying. All things are set into decay, not advancement. Even atheist scientists acknowledge the concept of entropy in the universe (the second law of thermodynamics). It explains that all things are bound to slow decay. This is hardly producing the self-composed utopia that New Age promises. It never will.

We can no longer afford to be uninformed on these topics. Our society is drowning in them unaware. These postulates are subtly laced into commercials, billboards, self-help books, and sermons. We must own the responsibility of a lucid response. We must clearly discern the lie in order to offer the truth. That is the task at hand; it is long overdue. The heart's longings that whisper from beneath New Age dogma are met in Christ. We have the answers they're looking for—the answers that New Age promises but cannot deliver. Let's move on from the condemnation and address those whispers . . . with a wink and a smile.

CHAPTER 6

# Energy in the Bible

*The definition of a "saint" —*
*A dead liberal who is revered by living conservatives.*

Invariably I am asked, "Can you show me *energy* in the Bible?" No, not directly. But then, I can't show you electricity or x-rays or "the Trinity" either. It would be a very different world if God gave us a scriptural reference for everything in life, but He clearly didn't choose to do that. The Bible is not an exhaustive encyclopedia, especially when it comes to the vast intricacies of creation. And to say that something is illegitimate or evil solely because it lacks a direct biblical reference is an inconsistent and weak argument. That said, there are several interesting theories about which Scriptures might hint at what physics is calling *energy*.

## Neshamah/Ruwach

When New Age says *energy*, believers say, "Ah yes, the *'breath of life.'*" God breathes the "life force" into us. The Bible describes the breath

97

of life by using a few different words. In Hebrew it most commonly uses the words *Neshamah* and *Ruwach*. *Neshamah* (nesh-aw-maw) is translated as a *puff*—i.e. wind, angry or vital breath, divine inspiration, intellect, or an animal blast, breath, soul, spirit. It is only used a few times in the canon, but I include it because it is the word used in Genesis 2:7 when . . . *the LORD God formed the man from the dust of the ground and breathed into his nostrils the **breath** of life, and the man became a living being.*

But most of the time when the Old Testament speaks of *the breath of life*, it uses the Hebrew word *Ruwach*. Pronounced "Roo-ahk," #7308 in *Strong's Concordance*, it means "spirit" or "breath". As spirit, it is used to denote the *Spirit* of God in the Old Testament and occasionally the *spirit* of a person or even an evil *spirit*.

As breath, it is used many times as the "breath of life" that God breathes into every living creature (humans and animals). It appears over 300 times in the Old Testament. When this breath is removed, we die. So, for living beings, this is a description of God's *vital energy*. The written name of God in Hebrew in the Old Testament doesn't have any vowels (actually none of written Hebrew has vowels). The four letters from which we derive our word *Yahweh* are actually four breathing sounds. The name of God—the sound of breathing. There are many scriptural references to this breath/*Ruwach* such as:

> *Genesis 1:30—"And to all the beasts of the earth and all the birds of the air and all the creatures that move on the ground—everything that has the breath of life in it—I give every green plant for food." And it was so.*

> *Deuteronomy 20:16—However, in the cities of the nations the LORD your God is giving you as an inheritance, do not leave alive anything that breathes.*

There are many *Ruwach* references to death, spoken as someone "breathing their last". I have found this to be the most typically held opinion of where Scripture alludes to *energy*. I would agree that it is the best description of what current culture would call life force. However, in the practicalities of Energy Psychology, I don't believe it is human *life force* that we are fundamentally dealing with.

## Chay

Another possibility for where the Bible references energy is in the Hebrew word *Chay* (pronounced "Kai"). It is #2416 in *Strong's Concordance* and it means "alive", "life", or "living" in the Hebrew. It is used in conjunction with the *Ruwach* Scriptures where it uses the phrase the *breath of life*. *Ruwach* is the "breath" and *Chay* is the "life." It commonly represents the idea of a whole life or lifespan, i.e., the six hundredth year of Noah's life (Gen. 7:11). Or when David says in Psalm 27:4, *One thing I ask of the LORD . . . that I may dwell in the house of the LORD all the days of my life.* So *Chay* refers not so much to life force per se but more to "a life". It describes the static rather than dynamic element of life.

## Pneuma

We continue on to the New Testament to find *Pneuma* (pronounced "Nooma", #4151) which means "breath" or "spirit." It is the New Testament equivalent to *Ruwach* and is more or less used in the same way. It would be the Greek description of "life force" or "breath of God".

But here is where I'm going to make a suggestion. I believe these words are useful descriptions of what New Age calls *vital energy*. But in Energy Psychology I think we need to discuss something else. We need to move one step further when we ask where the Bible might speak to this practice. Energy Psychology does not cause someone to be alive or dead. Energy Psychology influences the energy . . . adjusts it toward wholeness. Subsequently, I don't find the scriptural references we have so far addressed to be sufficient for our discussion.

## The Logos Argument

*Hebrews 1:3—The Son is the radiance of God's glory and the exact representation of his being, sustaining all things by his powerful word.*

As the quantum physicists explore things on this theoretical energetic level of creation, they discover something remarkable. Not only does thought and emotion seem to have some kind of substance on an energetic level as we discussed earlier, but thought, or intention, seems to *influence* energy. It seems that we human beings are constantly influencing the energetic field around us with our thoughts and emotions. It is as if our intentions feed into the energetic field. Our intention affects reality.

Here I am again in John 1. My heart keeps gravitating to this place. Over and over in those early years as I struggled to comprehend these issues, God seemed to take me back to this: *In the beginning was the Word, and the Word was with God, and the Word was God. He was with God in the beginning. Through him all things were made; without him nothing was made that has been made. In him was life and that life was the light of men.* This is a familiar and well-loved Scripture. We know that what we translate as Word in this passage is Logos in Greek. Logos (#3056 in *Strong's Concordance*) means, "something said or thought", "reasoning", "motive", "computation", or "divine expression". One afternoon while I studied this passage, I came across a remarkable commentary.

There has been a great deal of scholarly speculation about what John, in the prologue to his Gospel, meant by calling Jesus the Logos. It is not clear whether John meant to use it with its Greek or Jewish background in mind. His audience would have been familiar with both allusions. The Jewish background of Logos would have reminded his readers of the Genesis description of God "speaking" all of creation into existence and Psalm 33, where by the Word of the Lord the heavens were made. But it is the Greek background of the term Logos that is most interesting for our discussion. The commentary gives this description:

> *As a Greek philosophical term, logos referred to the "world-soul," that is, the soul of the universe. This was an all-pervading principle, the rational principle of the universe. It was a creative energy. In one sense, all things came from it; in another sense, people derived their wisdom from it. These concepts are at least as old as the Greek philosopher Heraclitus (6th century b.c.), who wrote that the logos is "always existent" and "all things happen through this logos." In later Hellenistic thought these concepts persisted but were modified somewhat. Philo of Alexandria, the Jewish philosopher of the early first century, frequently mentioned the logos (it appears over 1,400 times in his writings), but he was concerned with his Platonic distinction between this material world and the real, heavenly world of ideas. The Stoics, another group of Hellenistic philosophers, developed the concept of logos. For them it was the "force" that originated, permeated, and directed all things. It was the supreme governing principle of the universe. But the Stoics did not think of the logos as personal, nor did they understand it as one would understand God (i.e., as a person to be worshiped). In fact, they did not even think of single logos, but of logoi spermati koi ("seminal Reasons"), the forces responsible for the creative cycles in nature. Later Stoics considered the logos to be the "world-soul" in a pantheistic sense.[37]*

Isn't that incredible? If this historical reference is correct, John's audience may have known the word *Logos* like our culture knows the word *chi*. He was saying, "What you call the 'universal animating principal', 'life force', 'energy', I introduce to you as the *person* of Christ." God is not a force—He has personhood. Yes, we know that it is God who animates all things. He makes the molecules buzz. All things exist and live because He *wills* them to. But He has personhood. Even as early as Aristotle's day, they were aware that all things are in motion and that something must be *causing* that motion. Aristotle referred to this cause as "the unmoved mover". He describes the unmoved mover as being "perfectly beautiful, indivisible and contemplating only the perfect contemplation: itself contemplating". He equated this concept with what Thomas Aquinas called the "active intelligence".[38]

Similarly, Dr. Leslie Lyall, a Sinologist (expert on Chinese culture) and former director of the China Inland Mission, contends that the Chinese word *Tao* is derived from the same word as *The Word* in John 1 and *The Way* in John 14. They think of it as the first principle, "the universal cosmic energy behind the order of nature".[39] Like we might posit to the Chinese, John establishes for his audience in this one simple prologue that Jesus has full divinity and, upon becoming flesh, has full humanity. And it is His intention that sustains all things. "The God of the Bible is not a deistic clockmaker totally removed from creation; neither is creation fully comprehended by a narrow rationalism. Rather the universe is created and unified by Christ, the Logos . . . who personally directs and coordinates the richness of the cosmic drama without pantheistically merging with it" (John 1:1-14), (Col. 1:15-20), (Heb. 1:3).[40]

Dr. Phillip Johnson is quoted as saying:

> " . . . *energy healing opens up a mission field for Christians. Instead of apologists deconstructing or demonizing the field, they can follow Paul's mission paradigm of offering Christ as*

*the fulfillment of the pagan quest (Acts 17:16-34). Like Paul, the apologist can see from a creation-based theology that the Spirit is already behind the scenes preparing the spiritual harvest. Thus the apologist, armed with a fully fleshed theology of the Spirit of God in the creation, can say to a new age energy healer, 'what you call the universal life force, I now proclaim to you in its fullness is really the person of the Spirit of God who made you and commands us to repent.'"*

This is where I believe Scripture alludes most directly to what is happening in Energy Psychology. When God wanted to create the universe, He did not start working with His hands. He spoke. He willed. Physicists tell us that "matter" follows a particular set of rules. It is the following of those rules that *defines* something as matter. There is another set of rules that defines something as "information". One of the most incredible discoveries of quantum physics is that the infinitesimal particles we described earlier in Chapter 2 *actually follow the laws of information more than the laws of matter.*[41] Read that sentence again. It alone should blow your mind. At the core of all we call *matter* is actually information . . . thought . . . the intention and active will of God. Carl Sagan postulated that if you could get down to the core of the universe, you would find a mathematical equation. That's actually a good guess considering how God designed things to fit perfectly within the mathematical schema. But Sagan was wrong. At the core of all things is not an equation; it is thought. It is the active will of God "sustaining all things by his powerful word".

At the crucial point in human history, that *intention*, that will, that Logos became flesh and dwelt among us in order to sacrifice Himself in flesh to redeem us by His blood. What does it mean to be "made in the image" of this kind of God, Who sustains all things by His will? I am suggesting this: there is a great privilege and responsibility that comes with being made in His image. We have been given the profound honor of affecting things with our intention like He does, obviously on an infinitely smaller scale. He, of course, is sovereign. But in His sovereignty he has given us the ability to reign with Him. He has designed things so that we are meaningful players.

We know intuitively that what we think and feel and intend affects the world around us. And we know that in all of His creation we are unique in that quality. The rock doesn't impact its reality. It doesn't intend and change things. Even the animal in all its complexity and wonder does not reign. It merely follows the internal pre-designed "software" for its behavior. But God in His ultimate generosity and longing for partnership has afforded me *effect*. The quantum particles respond to my observation, to my thoughts. They reveal that He allows my every intention, my every thought and emotion to have weight . . . to make an impact. Not only do I have authentic free will, I am allowed to contribute ingredients into the cosmic soup. I am not just a responder to my world. I am a co-reigner in it. As human beings, we are all points of influence, whether or not we know Him who made it so. There is such a tendency to live as if we are mere observers of His sovereignty—as if we are purely responders. But it is not so. He intends and sustains the universe. He intends and reigns complete. I intend and reign in part. His will is constitutive. So is mine. Imago Dei.

Now let me be clear. I am not suggesting any trace of *equality* with God on this matter but allowance only. This is not remotely an *equal* partnership but a partnership none-the-less. Look at the canon itself. It begins and ends with the resounding call, "Reign with me!" God sets His image in His world and in essence says, "Subdue it, name it, fill it. Reign!" (Gen.1:28). He closes His Scriptures to us with the promise that those who have been faithful with little will now *reign with him* over much (2 Tim. 2:12, Mt. 25:14-29)! He tells us in Revelation that we will *reign for ever and ever* (Rev. 5:10, 22:5). He longs for relationship with us . . . for love

. . . for partnership. He wants this so deeply that He chooses to make His omnipotent self dependent on our partnership.

When I employ "circuitry + intention" and a client's traumatic emotion clears from their body on an energetic level, I am not manipulating their "life force". Their "breath of life" is God's alone to sustain and to remove. What I am doing is working intentionally within His established framework for reigning with Him. I am making grateful use of the privilege He has given me to affect the energetic level with my intention. I am being a meaningful player in the big story. I am being His hands and feet. By His design, my every thought and emotion are *always* impacting reality on an energetic level. When using these tools, I am simply doing it on purpose.

Throughout the Bible we read story after story of God's attempt to work *with* us, *through* us—to accomplish His purposes great and small in *partnership* with us. Logos describes how God wills or intends all things to exist and so they do. We are the only part of creation that has been given the profound honor of reason and consciousness. He has made us to have consciousness that is weighty . . . that is effective *partially*, as His own is effective *completely*. Our intention is meaningful. It is substantive.

Walter Bruggeman discusses this in depth in his scholarly work *Israel's Praise*.[42] He explores the fact that our speech and intention are creative/substantive—reflective of God's. We co-manage creation through our intention whether or not we acknowledge it as partnership with God, whether or not we acknowledge that what we are managing is *His*, and that we can only affect it because He allows us that honor.

When New Age dogma proclaims, "Look! Quantum physics proves that we control reality . . . that we are god!", believers have the opportunity that John had with his audience and that Paul had in Athens. We can say, "That energy that keeps the particles in motion . . . that sustains all things . . . is the very will of God. Let me introduce you to Him. His name is

Jesus. Not only are you not god, you are *responsible* for this grand privilege of affecting the particles with Him. You are *accountable*."

All of my life I have read those Scriptures: If there is anything lovely, anything praiseworthy . . . think on these things; take every thought captive; as a man thinks in his heart, so is he; you have heard it said, "Don't commit adultery", but I tell you, don't even go there in your heart . . . .. I heard all of these sorts of Scriptures like a big finger waving from the sky. "Be a good girl. Don't think bad things." It took quantum physics to show me that those were not just a big divine "Tsk, Tsk!" They were God saying, "It *matters* what goes on in your heart and mind. You reign with me with every emotion you feel . . . every thought you think. *Do it well!*"

New Age says, "You are *THE* creator." "Nothing exists unless you intend it." The *observation* that we affect reality is true. The *conclusion* that we are god is the problem. We need not throw out one to preserve the other. Yes, we influence reality. We affect the particles and participate in animating energy, but I am not sovereign. I am not the I Am. I am merely His privileged creature. The fact that New Age stretches this into apostasy doesn't mean I need to denounce the privilege. God says, "You are honored above all creation, made in My own image, capable of reigning with Me." The serpent says, "You are god."

It's the enemy's fatal twist on a wonderful truth.

But wonderful it remains.

# CHAPTER 7

# The Redemptive Posture

*"And, after all, what is a lie?*
*'Tis but the truth in a masquerade." —Alexander Pope*

*"All great truths begin as blasphemies."*
*—George Bernard Shaw*

Having established the stark differences between Christian doctrines and New Age creeds, it's now time to come at the discussion from the other side as well. Whether we like it or not, a good lie is effective because it's mostly true. Even New Age philosophy, believe it or not, is mostly true. That's why it's so seductive. A lie without any truth at all would be far too obvious and therefore ineffective. Our enemy knows that his lies must be big chunks of truth, laced with a tiny, crucial lie to help them go down smoothly. Our task here is to decipher where the truths are laced with lies. We take on that task because typically the Christian community does *not* do this. Generally believers do not maintain a redemptive stance in the face of falsehood. Instead, we tend to embrace one of two responses: we either reject the whole concept outright, truth included, or we accept it all and swallow truth *and* lie. Things are no different when it comes to the Christian community's response to New Age and to Energy Psychology. The most common response is to reject it as a whole.

It is for very good reason that Christians write off Energy Psychology as New Age. It is not an unfounded accusation. They are right. As a field, and in its philosophical underpinnings, it is almost entirely swallowed in New Age views. The problem comes in the Christian's assumption that *everything* New Age is false and therefore the whole "energy" concept must be evil by association.

We respond to New Age assertions as if we're hunkered down with our eyes closed and our fingers in our ears crying, "That's all evil!", rather than getting hold of ourselves and remembering that we are the children of the Creator of the Universe and that nothing observable in creation is inherently evil. Do we really believe we have discovered all there is to know about creation? Couldn't we still be surprised? Unfortunately Christians throughout history have a bad habit of adhering to the "Devil in the Gaps" theory when it comes to discovery.

In the 1980's and '90s as the evolution vs. creation debate was raging, Christians were being accused of the "God in the Gaps" theory. We were accused of crying, "That's supernatural", every time we couldn't explain or understand something. This did not give us credibility in the scientific community. Today, with energy we are doing the opposite. Because we can't see this energy under a microscope (yet), and because it operates in ways we don't understand, we automatically assume it's demonic. I propose that we're doing no better than usual. Not only do we undercut our credibility as rational thinkers and contributors to societal and scientific development, I believe we poorly represent God. Any time we come from a position of fear, we embarrass Him. All things are His. Because we know that and know Him, we should be the *first* to push the envelope, the boldest in discovery, and the loudest to shout out the mysteries and wonders of His inexhaustible creation. In fact, this used to be so. From Copernicus to

Galileo science was originally based on the assumption that God created things in an orderly manner; therefore it could be discovered and understood. Christians used to be the front-liners of discovery. The whole idea that faith and science are at odds is recent, unfounded, and lazy.

We don't ever have to react defensively to anything that can be observed in creation. And it is *observed*. It's not as if this energy only shows up in response to an incantation or the waving of a wand. Some form of this idea has been recognized and named respectively by nearly every culture throughout history. It is time we as believers lay down our defensive fear and remember that all things in heaven and earth belong to our God and that we can always afford to respond to scientific discovery with wonder and worship. Monty Kline coined the phrase "flat earth Christianity".[43] Medieval Christians believed that the earth was flat and that the suggestion that it was round was not only inaccurate but unchristian. It is a small view of our creator to act as if His truth is threatened by every new discovery we make of His own creation.

The other response is just as problematic. The other half of Christendom lands smack in the middle of the deception without considering the danger, all in the name of "everything is God's." They accept New Age as a whole without evaluating it critically through a biblical lens. Yoga is a great example of this. Many Christians have embraced America's new Yoga trend without a critical eye. They have not been wise in considering the background of Yoga or its potential spiritual underpinnings. If they practice under an orthodox Hindu teacher, even if that teacher is an American, they can naïvely place themselves under the influence of demonic forces involved in Hinduism. Originally, the poses of Yoga were intended to make one open to that particular "god". Yoga poses were intended to form the body like an antenna to attract and welcome that entity. Of course Yoga can certainly be found fully Westernized and neutered, but it can be found in its original form as well. Of course Yoga can and should be redeemed, but Christians have not always considered that it might take some closer attention in order to do that. My client who recommended the "What the Bleep" movie is another example. As New Age says, "all is one", Christians hear, . . . *in him and through him all things were made* and tumble right into one of that philosophy's most crucial errors. Martial arts is another example. Focused body control, self-defense, and discipline are wonderful things. But when our children are praying prayers to eastern gods to open and close karate practice, we have a problem. We must pay attention to where the lines are crossed.

We have established the lie element in each of the New Age tenets in order to avoid the former error. Now let's look at the truth in these tenets:

## Monism/Pantheism

*. . . sustaining all things by his powerful word . . .*
*(Heb. 1:3).*

All things exist in him and through him. *Without him nothing was made that has been made* (John 1:3). He holds the universe in His hands. The nugget of truth behind pantheism is the simplest to find. Of course God is in everything in the sense that things can only exist by His active, continuous *will*. It is Jesus for whom and through whom everything exists (Heb. 2:10). The particles are buzzing because He *wills* them to. He individually affords every breath I take. Yes, God is in everything— animating it, willing it to be, but those things are not the sum of Him. It is imperative that we grasp this seemingly subtle point. We must fiercely defend in our own minds the personhood, separateness, and hierarchy of the God of creation.

## Inner Divinity

*Christ in me, the hope of glory (Col. 1:27).*

God did design us to be glorious, to radiate in His image—to shine out to the world a piece of His glory and thereby call all the world to <u>Him</u>. But the New Age twist on this changes the whole story. Man seeks to *be* God rather than *reflect* God; glory set into man becomes the downfall of worship instead of its fuel. It is one thing to acknowledge that I have been "made in His image" and that I have the *mind of Christ* and the "spirit of truth". But it is entirely another to claim that presence as *myself*, dishonoring the gift as innate.

## Evolutionary Utopianism

*And we, who with unveiled faces all reflect the Lord's glory,*
*are being transformed into his likeness with ever-increasing*
*glory, which comes from the Lord, who is the Spirit*
*(2 Cor. 3:18).*

All things will be made new. We have an unparalleled hope in the place He is preparing for us, where the lion will lie down with the lamb and there will be no more tears or sorrow—where those of us who have been faithful with little will reign with Him over much. This story ends well. We win. But not through ourselves—quite in spite of ourselves. For who will deliver us from these bodies of death? Praise be to the Lord Jesus Christ, the author and perfecter of our faith! New Age preaches that by our own strength and wonderment we will propel ourselves into perfection. Scriptures say we *will be made new*. God will do this Himself. It will not be our own accomplishment as a species.

## Observation Vs. Conclusion

During those first years of investigation into all of this I was asking God every day to show me how *He* would have me approach things—how to keep from either extreme reaction to the New Age piece and respond with wisdom and authority. How could I respond in a way that would most honor Him?

As I continued to seek Him about how to use Energy Psychology tools to His glory, He began to show me where the boundary lines lie between these two extremes. The surprise was that those lines tended to land more around conclusion than practice. I expected Him to show me that I had to take what New Agers were doing and change it around in some fundamental way, or that only a handful of techniques could pass the test and the rest had to be thrown out. But I was surprised to find that practice was not typically the central problem. The problems that one needed to be wary of in order to maneuver in this field of Energy Psychology and maintain spiritual soundness were usually those of *philosophy*. The observations that are being made about the energetic level of things are not against God in any way. How could anything we observe in His creation be offensive to faith? We need to separate what is observed from what is concluded. The rub is not in observation but in philosophy—in *conclusion*.

In our example, physics observes that there seems to be something like energy at the core of everything, at the smallest level of creation, because everything is in motion. Physicists also observe that everything at the smallest level seems to be made up of the same fluid, interdependent stuff. Now up until this point we don't have a theological issue. We have merely observed something in God's creation . . . a creation that He calls completely *good*. Anything observable in creation just shows off God's unsearchable works. The trouble starts when New Age draws critically incorrect *conclusions* from these observations.

Physicists reason that since this energy is at the core of all things, unifying and animating all things, *it must be god* . . . therefore, the rock is god, the tree is god, I am god, etc. If one is predisposed to reject the truth of a personal God, it would be convenient to conclude from these observations that an impersonal force of energy underlies and organizes the universe. And if that very force makes up one's self, then I am at least part of god, if not all. The jump from energy to divinity is a short one for the unchecked human ego.

The problem for a believer is not in the observation of this energy at the core of everything; it is with the conclusion drawn from it that we are God. The problem is in conclusion, not observation. We need not deny that something like energy is buzzing around at the core of things in order to uphold Christianity. We *do* need to deny the New Age conclusion that says, "Therefore I am god." It is not a stretch from a biblical worldview to say that this energy could very well be there without undoing the sovereignty or separateness of God in any way. It is God, of course, who *causes* the molecules to buzz. Dr. Groothuis states it this way:

> *"A biblical cosmology is not offended by modern speculations on the unity and interconnection of creation. While we must view such scientific theories with caution, the Bible pictures a God who sustains and unifies creation without violating the created integrity of distinct entities. Rather than a monistic cosmology, the biblical view of creation harmonizes the one (unity of creation) with the many (distinct creations). The biblical view, then, is holistic without being monistic."*[44]

We discussed earlier that quantum physics suggests that observation affects the quantum particles . . . that only upon observation do they shift from potential into actualization in the form of either wave or particle. This *observation* has led to the New Age philosophy we've discussed earlier— that nothing actually exists unless I think it does, or at least until I observe it. Undeniably, this is an overreaction to long-held scientific determinism that grew out of the Newtonian, classical model. Classical physics inaccurately painted the universe as a closed system—a locked elaborate machine with no room for either free will or the intervention of a sovereign God. But the New Age philosopher jerks his knee and makes the opposite mistake that human intention is the sole universal causal force. But our problem is not with the *observation* of properties at the quantum level, only with New Age *conclusions* about it.

This postulate of finding the boundary lines in conclusion vs. observation is useful on most fronts. Generally, the observations underpinning Energy Psychology (and other fields of energy work) are not faulty and are not even inherently moral. They are just descriptions of how things seem to operate both within the energy field of things and in the connection between mind and body. The observations are merely describing what is happening, just as the laws of gravity describe what is going on when an apple falls to the ground. The problem begins for a believer when observations lead to *conclusions* that undercut the basics of a biblical worldview.

Another example of this observation vs. conclusion rule of thumb is how New Age presents the subconscious mind. It starts with the observation that the subconscious mind has remarkable awareness and remarkably detailed data about one's life experiences. This is true. The subconscious is far more aware than the conscious mind and it does have an exhaustive database on our lives. The subconscious database is truly remarkable, but as usual, the problem for a believer comes in when New Age draws its *conclusions* from this observation. It concludes that awareness is commensurate with wisdom. They make the jump from data to judgment. They posit that since the subconscious mind has this amazing awareness and data, it must be our center of all wisdom . . . our divine knowing of all things. It teaches that if we could just learn to access this subconscious wisdom center, we could literally know everything. It is even called the "Christ consciousness". But it requires only a cursory investigation to find the hole in this argument. The subconscious has good data and poor judgment.

For instance, the subconscious mind knows that at age 5, I felt betrayed and abandoned. It does not know that my parents were only going for an innocent weekend alone together. Its judgment center is thoroughly biased. It knows only its own reactions and impressions. My subconscious knows I do not feel completely safe around the man I'm dating. It does not know whether he is a good choice for me to marry. I may feel unsafe because of simple fears of commitment. My subconscious only knows "unsafe".

So here again, the boundary line falls on conclusion, not observation. Yes, the subconscious mind does have a remarkable database and is far more aware than the conscious mind. My deep soul has a record of everything I have ever thought or felt. But the truth is that the subconscious is very fear-based and infantile in judgment. It is the part of us that chooses our symptoms. The conscious mind doesn't ever choose symptoms. Consciously we choose life. But the subconscious chooses the fear-based response every time. Now of course there can be physical factors involved in psychological symptoms, but it is arguable that even what shows up as physical can be a *response* to emotional roots rather than the cause.

Unfortunately, it is the subconscious that chooses symptoms, because it is that part of us that is drawing harmful associations between our past traumas and our current experiences. It is the subconscious that opts for faulty coping strategies and self-sabotage of all creative varieties. So yes, the observation that the subconscious has an incredible database is correct. The conclusion that it is therefore our center of all wisdom is false; that's where the boundary line needs to be drawn.

Let's apply this to Chakra work. Do energy centers exist along the body's midline? Probably. There is the observation piece. So far we are in theologically neutral territory. That observation is not inherently moral.

The trouble arises in the conclusion drawn by those who first observed these centers. Because they already had a monistic worldview, they interpreted that observation, unavoidably, through that lens and concluded that these must represent man's inner divinity in dormant potential for godhood. The alignment and opening of these energy centers, they reasoned, would probably facilitate the manifestation of that divinity.

Observation = neutral.

Conclusion = deceptive.

Because Energy Psychology is such a new field, I've been unable to find anything written on it from a Christian perspective. There are a few references on energy medicine, however, since it's far more prolific and a bit older. One of the better resources I found in my research was Neil Anderson and Michael Jacobson's *The Biblical Guide to Alternative Medicine*. It covers a wide range of practices and issues evenhandedly. They caution the reader throughout the book to be aware of the philosophical and theological origins of energy medicine practices, proposing that those origins render the practices unacceptable to the Christian. But after all of the warnings, they state

> *"There are those who warn that pagan-based practices . . . cannot be separated from their occult roots, and that submitting oneself to such practices makes one vulnerable to the occult. However, this is probably also related to the spiritual maturity of the client and their uncompromising faith in God and His Word. Separation can and does occur. Christians are like Western medical practitioners and scientists who are atheists but still study God's creation— thereby discovering general revelation. They can separate a*

*physical treatment in the natural realm, a false pagan interpretation from the treatment and a practitioner's false beliefs from the Word of God in order to receive treatments without leaving themselves vulnerable to demonic forces. However, we recommend that you pray before, during and after the treatment and that you not submit to any procedure that bypasses your conscious state of mind."*[45]

The main argument in Christendom against the use of these kinds of tools is that they are off limits based on their philosophical roots. But there is a little hypocrisy in this argument. We would be hard-pressed to find anything that can trace its roots purely to biblical foundations. The entire field of medicine is rooted in the worship of Greek gods. The famous Hippocratic Oath, originally required to be sworn by all medical practitioners, begins as follows:

*"I swear by Apollo Physician and Asclepius and Hygieia and Panaceia and all the gods and goddesses, making them my witnesses, that I will fulfill according to my ability and judgment this oath and this covenant:"*

It ends accordingly with this superstition:

*"If I fulfill this oath and do not violate it, may it be granted to me to enjoy life and art, being honored with fame among all men for all time to come; if I transgress it and swear falsely, may the opposite of all this be my lot."*[46]

No one can deny, however, that current culture has well divorced the practice of modern medicine from these errant "roots". Christians do not villainize the practice of modern medicine because of these philosophical origins; well they shouldn't. Similarly, the fact that the concept of energy arose in the East does not disqualify it as true or as God's.

Can an eastern person not find *any* general truth? Is a non-Christian unable to observe anything in creation correctly just because they don't know the living God? It is a logical error to say that observation and philosophy are inseparable. An unbeliever can of course correctly observe something in creation. It is unavoidable, yes, that he will interpret it through his worldview, but that worldview can be removed from the observation. No matter what my worldview, I cannot help interpreting any observation through that lens. I have no other choice. I cannot know what I do not know. But someone else, with a different worldview, can surely sift the observation from my lens, even if I cannot. If I believe the world is flat, I may accurately observe that a ship disappears at the horizon. My lens affords me no other interpretation but that the sailors are lost into oblivion. But if another comes along who knows that the earth is round, *he doesn't have to deny observation, only my conclusion.* In order to uphold his worldview, he does not have to deny that the ship does disappear, only where it has gone. If missionaries worked with a tribe of Aborigines who believed that a demonic force caused an apple to fall from a tree, it wouldn't therefore become incumbent upon the Christians to deny that apples fall.

The argument commonly made is that because these ideas are rooted in pantheism, they are to be rejected. But we need to acknowledge that *when* these were birthed, those people groups were pre-Cross and did not have any revelation of the true God other than nature itself, from which they formed pantheism. The observation and conclusion not only *can* be separated . . . but *must* be. Otherwise we leave ourselves with only two options: either we deny that apples fall, saying that what every human culture throughout history has observed and described doesn't really exist . . . or we actually go so far as to say that it is inherently evil . . . that it belongs to the enemy. Are we really willing to do that?

Check in with your gut at this point. What do you notice? What reactions arise? Where do you hear old voices and religious traditions cropping up? It is, of course, impossible for any of us to hear anything with pure objectivity (myself included). We hear everything through our pre-designed frameworks—through our lenses. But what if we didn't? What if we could peer around the side of our lens for just a moment? Would we find that He is less than we thought or more? Would we find His reach stretching longer or shorter? What if redemption waits pregnant in every corner of reality? Could we see it?

We have established the basics of New Age—its lies and its truths. Now we'll look at witchcraft.

CHAPTER 8

# The Basics of Witchcraft

*"Times may change, the programmes may sound different, but again and again occult prophets promise to man the things he dreams of." —Samuel Pfeifer, in* Healing At Any Price?

*What's the best thing about your Wiccan girlfriend?*
*She worships the ground you walk on.*

T he Christian Research Institute at www.equip.org is quoted as saying,

" . . . *we find no solid reason to believe that the energy of energetic [medicine] is physical and scientific, but several good reasons to strongly suspect that if it exists at all . . . it is supernatural and demonic. The risk is great, therefore, that it cannot be utilized without the utilizer becoming the utilized (i.e., a pawn and victim of satanic forces and deception). In fact, . . . research of occultism . . . suggests that this energy is part and parcel of the occult—where the occult appears it can be found; where it is found, the occult will inevitably appear."*

—Elliot Miller, 2009[47]

We have addressed the first accusation against the Christian's use of Energy Psychology: it is New Age. Now let's turn our attention to the second accusation: that it is witchcraft. Again, in order to establish grounds for our discussion, we need to define our vernacular. What is witchcraft?

We have several terms here to navigate. The most commonly used are: *witchcraft, occultism, Satanism, divination, sorcery,* and *magic.* For our purposes let's set aside the practice of Satanism (formal Satanic rituals), because it is a rare Christian who would accuse another believer working with Energy Psychology of doing overt, intentional worship of Satan. That renders it mostly irrelevant to our conversation. The other terms we will lump together under the global term *witchcraft* for simplicity. *Harper's Bible Dictionary* defines a *witch* as "a specialist in the manipulation of intangible powers of evil against people".[48] Under the heading "magic and divination" they give this definition: "means by which humans attempt to secure for themselves some action or information from superhuman powers. Magic is an attempt by human beings to compel a divinity, by the use of physical means, to do what they wish that divinity to do. Divination is an attempt to secure information, also by the use of physical means, about matters and events that are currently hidden or that lie in the future."[49] In New Testament Greek it is:

μαγεύω; μαγεία, ας *f*: to practice magic, presumably by invoking supernatural powers—'to practice magic, to employ witchcraft, magic.'[50]

Neil Anderson and Michael Jacobson suggest in their book *The Biblical Guide to Alternative Medicine* that there are three salient characteristics of a practice that involves contact with the occult:

1. The purpose of the activity is to gain information or power.

2. The immaterial (i.e. the spirit, supernatural, or energy realm) is asked to manifest itself (i.e. give an answer) through a material object.

3. The question is usually (but not always) framed so as to obtain a simple yes or no answer.[51]

The biblical world, with its primitive understanding of science, strove to make sense of the mysterious and unknown (as we still do today). They had an elaborate construct to connect the supernatural and divine with the mundane. The word *magic* is derived from the Persian word *magus*, where it designated a priestly class. Magical practices have been recorded in every human civilization known to history. P. J. Achtemeier describes the general principles upon which the practice of magic was based:

> *"A host of intermediary beings called demons were thought to exist between gods and humans. Depending on their proximity to the gods, demons possess divine power in diminishing measures. Those closest to the gods have bodies of air; those closest to humans, bodies of steam or water. Because of this descending order, the unity of the cosmos can be preserved. Otherwise, human and divine would be irreparably separated and no communication between the two would be possible. Everything is connected through the demons who mediate between the divine and the material. Magic rests upon the belief that by getting hold of demons in physical objects, the divinity can be influenced. The magician's art is to find out which material (metal, herb, animal, etc.) contains which divinity and to what degree. By using the element or combinations of elements containing a particular divinity in its purest form, a sympathetic relationship with the divinity will be established. If, however, elements offensive to a divinity are used, the result will be antipathetic. Thus magic*

*can achieve either blessing or curse. The magician knows the secret and knows how to use it in the correct way with the best results."*[52]

Regardless of whether a particular person or culture adheres to that sort of a worldview, there remains one common theme in all of the practices of witchcraft throughout culture and time. That commonality will be our definition.

*Witchcraft is the attempt to gain special knowledge or power outside of God.*

What do we mean by "special"? We mean power or knowledge that is not found or allowed by God in the natural order. For instance, the pursuit of special knowledge could look like the use of any means to know the future—a practice clearly condemned in Scriptures such as Deuteronomy 18:10, Isaiah 47:13, and several others. Special knowledge can also be more subtle, like the pursuit of direction. Should I take the job in Atlanta or Chicago? Is this a good business risk?

Special power is more obvious. The cliché example is crooned over in the popular 1950's song, "Love Potion #9", in which the singer is pining for a way to secure his sweetheart's affections. A person may pursue the power to harm or bless another or to control their actions. They may also pursue power over events—i.e. financial prosperity or a rain dance.

Scripture gives many accounts of witchcraft in its different styles and many harsh admonishments to abstain from it.

Witchcraft (Deut. 18:10)
Sorcery (Deut. 18:10)
Fortune-telling (Deut. 18:10)
Communicating with spirits (Deut. 18:11)

Mediums (Deut. 18:11)
Divination (Deut. 18:10)
Astrology (Deut. 4:19; Isa. 47:13-15)
Heresy (false teaching) (1 Tim. 4:1; 1 John 4:1-3)
Immorality (Eph. 2:2-3)
Self-deification (Gen. 3:5; Isa. 14:12)
Lying (John 8:44)
Idolatry (1 Cor. 10:19-20)
Omens (Num. 24:1)
Oracles (Num. 24:3)[53]

All of these are pursuits either of special knowledge, special power, or a combination of the two.

## Special Knowledge

The biblical catch-all term for the pursuit of special knowledge is *divination*. The word used is *Kasam* (קסם, LXX μαντεύω). It stands for Joseph's divining cup. The original meaning of the word seems to be "to divide" or "partition out". Its first appearance is where the elders of Moab go to Balaam *taking with them the fee for divination* (Num. 22:7) and where the seer announces that there is *no divination against Israel* (23:23). Balaam is directly called a *diviner* (A.V. *soothsayer*) in Josh. 13:22. We meet with it among the list of similar practices in Deut. 18:10 and 14, where we are given to understand that it was common among the Canaanites.[54] Ancient peoples used several means for "divining" information. The *New Bible Dictionary* lists the following forms that are mentioned in Scripture:

*Rhabdomancy*—(Ezek. 21:21). Sticks or arrows were thrown into the air, and omens were deduced from their position when they fell (Hos.

4:12). Similar was the watching of the flights of birds in order to determine the immediate future.

*Hepatoscopy*—(Ezek. 21:21). Examination of the liver or other entrails of a sacrifice was supposed to give guidance. Similar to this was the observing of the eating patterns of chickens!

*Teraphim*—Household idols were consulted for information/guidance, and are associated with divination in 1 Samuel 15:23, Ezekiel 21:21, and Zechariah 10:2. If the teraphim were images of dead ancestors, the divination was probably a form of spiritualism. In Acts 16:16 a girl has a spirit of divination. The Greek here is *pythōn*. There was a famous Delphic oracle in the district of Pytho; the term evidently was used loosely for anyone supernaturally inspired, as she was. Formal statues of gods were also consulted somehow, such as the Memnon at Thebes.[55]

*Necromancy, or the consultation of the dead*—This is associated with divination in Deuteronomy18:11, 1 Samuel 28:8, and 2 Kings 21:6, and is condemned in the Law (Lev. 19:31; 20:6), the Prophets (Isa. 8:19–20), and the historical books (1 Chron. 10:13). The medium was spoken of as having an ʾ*ôḇ*, translated "a familiar spirit", or in modern terms "a control". An associated term, translated *wizard*, is *yidʿôni*, probably from the root *yāḏaʿ*, meaning know, presumably refers to the supernatural knowledge claimed by the spirit and in a secondary sense by its owner. The infamous "witch of Endor" was a necromancer, conjuring "familiar spirits" for information and guidance. Another common way the gods were thought to communicate was through the wind blowing in the leaves of an oak tree. There were several famous oak trees such as those of Dodona where omens could be obtained.[56]

*Astrology*—Astrology draws conclusions from the position of the sun, moon, and planets in relation to the zodiac and to one another.

*Lecanomancy/Hydromancy, or divination through water*—Here forms and pictures appear in the water in a bowl, as also in crystal gazing.

The gleam of the water induces a state of light trance; the visions are subjective. The only reference to this in the Bible is Genesis 44:5 and 15, where it might appear that Joseph used his silver cup for this purpose.

*Lots*—Similar to the modern practice of drawing straws, with the assumption that supernatural intervention with the straws would cause an intended outcome.

*Dreams*—Dreams are often counted as a means of divination (Jer. 23:25–27).[57]

*Oracles*—These were individuals who were thought to receive messages from the gods through different means. The oracle "Pythia" of Delphi is one of the best known.[58]

For each of these forms, the common theme is the pursuit of knowledge/information outside of the natural order.

## Special Power

The other main pursuit underlying witchcraft is special power. In order to gain these powers, many instruments and practices used in biblical times are still used today. Some examples are charms, amulets, spells, rituals, and the use of proxy. The Hebrew word interpreted *sorcery* in Scripture (*kšp̄*) probably literally means "to cut" and refers to the cutting of herbs or plants for the preparation of charms and potions. All of these were employed in order to cause a specific effect outside of one's natural influence (not unlike modern pharmacology). For instance, a spell might be arranged to cause an enemy to become deathly ill. An amulet was worn because it would keep the bearer safe (ironically from the witchcraft of others). A charm was also an object, believed to be instilled with supernatural blessing, that would be worn or carried. Proxy involved creating some kind of representation of another person and doing spells, curses, hexes, or physical damage to that object, intending the same thing to befall the actual individual, e.g. voodoo dolls.

## Combinations

King Nebuchadnezzar is an example of the combination of the two. He engaged witchcraft in order to know how to proceed in battle (special knowledge) so that he could ensure victory (special power). "He used three means to determine his course of action: casting lots with arrows, consulting his idols, and examining the liver. Casting lots with arrows was probably similar to today's practice of drawing straws. Two arrows were placed in a quiver, each one inscribed with the name of one of the cities being considered for attack. The arrow drawn or cast out first was the one the gods indicated should be attacked. The consulting of "idols" (ter pîm) involved the use of teraphim or household idols. The exact nature of this practice is unknown, but perhaps the idols were used in an attempt to contact departed spirits and hear their advice. Examining the liver was a form of divination known as *hepatoscopy*. The shape and markings of the liver of a sacrificed animal were studied by soothsayers to see if a proposed plan was favorable or not."[59]

## "White" Witchcraft

*"Eight words the Wiccan Rede fulfill: An' it harm none,
Do what ye will . . ."—The Wiccan Rede*

*"Contrary to what those who choose to persecute or lie about
us wish to believe, Wicca is a very peaceful, harmonious and
balanced way of life which promotes oneness with the divine
and all which exists."*
*—Wicca.com*

The scriptural injunctions against witchcraft in its various forms make no distinction between "black" or "white" witchcraft. It does not seem to matter whether one intends to do good or evil. If a person is pursuing special knowledge or power outside of God, they are in sin, even if their intention is to bless. Wicca, the modern-day nomenclature for "white" witchcraft, holds dear the intention to do only good, never harm. But turning to an ultimate source outside of God is still the issue. Whether one intends to do good or harm, there are two elements present in the practice of witchcraft.

As we have discussed, there is the pursuit of special knowledge or power outside of God. That we could classify generally as rebellion. *"Rebellion is like the sin of divination"* (1 Sam. 15:23). But there is another issue at hand. Idolatry. One can be involved in the pursuit of special knowledge/power and not overtly involved in idolatry. For instance, a person can believe that reading tea leaves or their horoscope will give them information about their immediate future. They are not consciously pursuing a supernatural *entity* for information. I would argue that they are still *employing* a supernatural entity but not on purpose. On the other hand, witchcraft and Wicca both give great homage to the god and goddess of nature. In their pursuit of power and knowledge they are intentionally calling on the involvement of those entities and their supposed underlings.

The issue at the heart of witchcraft is not whether one means it for good or evil or even whether one is aware that they are employing demonic involvement. The issue is both rebellion and idolatry when supernatural power sources are consciously invoked and at least rebellion when they are not. The Farrars, in *A Witches Bible Compleat*, purport that the Judeo-Christian, Monotheistic God never has existed. It was man-made for political reasons and social control. Basically "You made up that God." Which, ironically is the same accusation we have against them . . ."You made up that goddess. It has never really existed." They work hard to prove that priests and priestesses of all genuine religions (*genuine* defined as having a core purpose of pushing the human consciousness upward in development, i.e. meaning to bless) are all colleagues. They exhibit great respect for all religions, because we all know we're "aligned at the same peak".[60] And . . . we're back to New Age.

I can't help taking a little sidebar here to say that we give the enemy far too much credit. The truth is that the occult is *not* very powerful. Ninety percent of what they try to do fails. Psychics, for instance, do not have a good track record. *The People's Almanac* (1976) did a study of the predictions of 25 top psychics, including Dixon. The results: "Out of the total 72 predictions, 66 (or 92 percent) were dead wrong" (Kole, 69). Of those correct to some degree, two were vague and two hardly surprising— the United States and Russia would remain leading powers and there would be no world wars. It is clear that it does not take supernatural powers to get these subnormal results."[61] Pharaoh had his magicians, but even they marveled at Moses, saying, *"This is the finger of God!"* (Ex. 8:19).

Witchcraft is not all its cracked up to be.

# CHAPTER 9

# Redemption in Witchcraft?

## (Surely not!)

She's worried about me. She asks me again, "Can we sit down and talk?" My cousin is a sharp thinker and deeply devoted to the Lord. She has watched my career from afar, and she's afraid for my holiness. She wants to be able to trust my walk with God. She hopes that if we hash it through a little further, she can see my position more clearly. We steal away and sit down around a dusty little picnic table in Yosemite Valley, where my family gets together each summer. She draws an imaginary line down the middle of the table. She says, "I feel like if this is the line, you live right up next to it." "Yes, that's right," I say. (She expected me to argue with that.) "But it seems to me that if the line is there, we should live back here" (drawing her hands close to her body). I understand what she's saying . . . "Be safe!" she's thinking. "Live far from any possibility of trouble." I pause, carefully choosing my words. "So, did God draw the line in the wrong place?" "Was He too conservative?" "It really should've been back there?" She thinks . . . I continue . . . "What about all the *life* in between?" I went on to assure her that I'm very aware of the weight of where I choose to stand. I do not take it lightly. I live every day under the pressure and responsibility of calling believers up against that line. It is no small thing.

But due to further studying of Scripture, something significant has changed since that conversation—something that has surprised me. It was many years ago that I went through the work of answering the first question: "How would you do this work without getting into New Age?" I was long familiar with those boundary issues: hold fast to the personhood and hierarchy of God. But when it came time to write this book, I had to deal with the second major accusation . . . witchcraft. Truthfully, I couldn't intelligently address the question, "How is this different from witchcraft?", because I didn't know enough *about* witchcraft and how it works. I can't argue that I'm not doing witchcraft when I don't know what witchcraft is. I am confident that God has led my life in this direction, but "I just know" is not an argument.

## The Heart of Witchcraft

During my third pregnancy I had to spend a week in the hospital. Seven days of quiet and solitude, nothing to do—a rare experience for a mother of two toddlers. I decided to spend the time doing the dreaded task at hand . . . researching witchcraft. I knew that God had directed me to do this a while earlier, but I had been procrastinating. I can't tell you how many times I had to explain myself to the uncomfortable nurse who had just come in to take my blood pressure and seen my stack of black books covered in pentagrams. "Not a witch," I would assure them. "Just doing research." It made for a few funny moments.

I wanted to go to the foundation. I wanted to hear what a *witch* would tell me about witchcraft, not a Christian commentary. I read the six or so publications considered to be the "bibles" of witchcraft—the orthodox sources, pentagrams and all. What I found was perplexing. Years earlier, when I looked deeply into New Age, I expected to find clear lines in practice. I thought I would learn how to show someone that "this practice is godly and this one is New Age," but as we have discussed, that is not what I found. It turned out that the issue was not so much with a particular practice but with a posture of heart. It was more about being clear on *who* God is.

But this time, coming to witchcraft, *surely* the lines will be obvious. This will be a no-brainer. Witchcraft . . . bad. We know that God abhors witchcraft. Scriptures are clear about this. Most of us are familiar with the oft-quoted *"Thou shalt not suffer a witch to live"* (Ex. 22:18, KJV). But once again my study was perplexing. What I found inside those dusty black covers is that witchcraft in its philosophical origins is surprisingly altruistic. There was no mention or acknowledgment anywhere of demons, evil, Satan, etc. They consider themselves aligned with the divinity inherent in nature—with the god and goddess of the earth/universe whom they consider to be benevolent and equal in authority with one another though different in sphere.

They would say it's preposterous and superstitious to suggest that they are aligned with "the devil". They are not aware, apparently, that the supernatural sources they are invoking are demonic. Their experience of these gods seems to be positive. When these witchcraft manuals talk of their "craft", there is an overriding theme of love, celebration, harmony with nature, and the pursuit of overall improvement for the earth and the human race. As far as their *intentions* (other than straying in the universal human sense such as selfishness or materialism), they are generally well-meaning. There is the occasional ill will toward another, but it is the exception to the rule and still not considered by them to be aligned with evil *per se* but more with justice.

So that research didn't help me much. I was more confused than *before* I studied witchcraft. Witchcraft is sin. It's indisputable. I am by no means defending witchcraft, but I didn't know how to make sense of what I had read, so I went back to the Word. And again, I was surprised at what I found. Remember our list of witchcraft elements in the last chapter? Look at this next list:

## Biblical Practices

Aaron was shown to be God's choice as priest when his rod budded (Num. 17).[62]

The flight of arrows foretold a victory to King Joash (2 Kings 13:14-19).

Joseph interpreted the dreams of Pharaoh (Gen. 41) and Daniel those of Nebuchadnezzar by the power of God (Dan. 2, 4). Joseph, husband of Mary, received God's messages in dreams (Mt. 1:20-21; 2:13), as did the wise men (Mt. 2:12) and Pilate's wife (Mt. 27:19).

Scripture records for us the visions of Samuel in the Temple (1 Sam. 3), Peter's vision in Acts 10, and several other examples. Visions, mostly from the Lord, were so widespread that the word is used in the Revised Standard Version of the Bible more than one hundred times.

The *Magi*, the *wise men* of Matthew 2, and the *Chaldeans* of Daniel 1 and 2 had priestly functions. Daniel was made *chief of the magicians* because *"the spirit of the holy gods . . . light and understanding and wisdom, like the wisdom of the gods"*, were found in him (Dan. 5:11, KJV). God allowed the Magi, non-Jewish priestly magicians, to play a significant role in heralding the newborn Messiah by following astronomical signs. The Magi were non-Jewish religious astrologers.[63]

Exodus 8:5-9:12 tells the familiar story of God enabling Moses to outdo the Egyptian magicians in their own tricks.

During the early history of Israel, it was an accepted practice to *inquire of the Lord* (Judg. 1:1-2; 1 Sam. 10:22). This expression implies an oracle (similar to Delphi in Greece) where a question could be asked and a reply given by God through some sort of tool. The most scholarly acknowledged form of "tool" for receiving answers from God was known as the Urim and Thummim described in 1 Samuel 23:9-12, 30:7-8 and Numbers 27:21. The high priest of Israel wore a breastplate with 12 stones on it—one to represent each of the tribes of Israel. On top of that was a small bag called the *ephod*. It contained two stones, the Urim and Thummim. When people wanted to *inquire of the Lord*, they would come to the High Priest and ask God a question. As far as scholars can ascertain (since the biblical accounts are brief), it seems that God would cause one or the other of the stones to light up indicating a "yes" or "no" answer. Apparently, the use of the Urim and Thummim is sometimes indicated by the term *ephod* (1 Sam. 23:9-12, 30:7-8), by reference to the Ark of the Covenant (Judg. 20:27; 1 Sam. 14:18), and by the phrase *ask of God* (1 Sam. 23:2, 4).[64]

Isn't that incredible?

Exodus 13:9, 16 and Deuteronomy 6:8 and 11:18 recount God's direction to wear phylacteries on their hands and foreheads. Matthew 23:5 describes them being worn by Pharisees.

Elijah's mantle parted the waters of the Jordan; Elisha put it on, Elijah's spirit rested on him (2 Kings 2:8-15). The garment of Jesus radiated and transmitted healing power (Mark 5:28-29), as did the handkerchiefs and aprons that people carried away from the body of Paul (Acts 19:11-12). Some first-century believers even attributed beneficial properties to the shadow of Peter (Acts 5:15).[65]

Sampson's uncut hair holds supernatural power given by God that was lost when it was cut (Judg. 16).

Elijah could heal the son of the widow of Zarephath by stretching himself upon the child three times in 1 Kings 17:17-24. The same miracle was repeated by Elisha with the son of the Shunamite in 2 Kings 4:31-37.

The Holy Spirit was given through the laying on of the apostles' hands; this was the secret the magician Simon wished to learn (Acts 8:9-24).

God's Old Testament Law taught that contact with unclean objects would cause an individual to become unclean himself; hence the many purificatory rites. Purification was achieved by the use of the correct rites and materials, among which particular power was attributed to animal blood (Lev. 14:25), water (Lev. 15:5), fire (Num. 31:23), but also to hyssop, scarlet thread, and many other agents (Ps. 51:7; Num. 19:18; Lev. 14:4).

In Genesis 30:37 Jacob appears to be able to cause his livestock to reproduce in a special way by placing striped sticks in front of them while they eat.

Curse and blessing are portrayed in Deborah's song (Judg. 5) and referred to many times throughout the Scriptures as part of God's design. David's reluctance to interfere with Shimei in 2 Samuel 16 is based on the fear that God may have inspired the curse for something that David had done.[66]

Near the land of Edom, God instructed Moses to fashion a bronze serpent and place it on a pole. God used this as an instrument in saving the lives of the people. They were told that if they looked at it, they would be healed (Num. 21:4-9; 2 Kings 18:4; cf. John 3:14-15).

Various notable events recorded in the Bible were determined righteously by the casting of lots. Saul, Israel's first king, was selected in this manner (1 Sam. 10:16-26). The conquered land was apportioned among the tribes by lot (Num. 26:55; Josh. 14:2). The identity of Achan as the thief of the spoil from Jericho was discovered by lot (Josh. 7:14). By this means Jonathan was found to be the (unwitting) violator of his father's oath (1 Sam. 14:42). The ranks of Temple personnel were also determined by lot (1 Chron. 24:5; 25:8; 26:13; cf. Luke 1:9). Matthias was chosen in this way to replace Judas among the 12 apostles (Acts 1:26).[67]

Isn't that an amazing list? Isn't it a little confusing? I could even have made it considerably longer (See Appendix A). Regardless of how they seem, *these are not accounts of sin*. They are accounts of the people of God operating within His blessing. They are not accounts of witchcraft. But don't they sound like they are? If someone told you today that if you wore blue every day throughout your pregnancy, you would be guaranteed to have a boy, what would your first reaction be? Would you think, "Yes, that sounds godly"? If someone explained to you that their finances were in shambles because they were under a curse, what would you think? What if they told you that they had supernatural power as long as they don't cut their fingernails or that if you wear a scarlet thread, you will be purified before God? There are many things in Scripture that are endorsed by God that would seem like witchcraft in another context. Over and over Scripture condemns witchcraft, calling it an abomination. And yet we have examples like these where the very same kinds of structures are employed within righteousness. How do we make sense of that? If the behaviors themselves can be righteous acts, what is it that makes something witchcraft?

*What makes something witchcraft is not a particular act. It is the idolatry and rebellion behind those acts.*

## The Real Line

We want to be able to draw the line *behaviorally*. We want there to be "safe zone" and "evil zone"—safe acts and evil ones. We want to be able to evaluate life and say, "Over here in these practices I'm in God's camp. I can relax. And over there in those practices is the enemy's camp. Those behaviors are off limits. As long as I don't engage in those behaviors, I'm in good shape with God." We want the lines to be clear and simple, but they are not. Neither safe zone nor evil zone is real. I can be singing a hymn and have my mind and heart in the most evil posture imaginable. I can be prophesying, as Scripture shows us multiple times, from the Spirit of God or a demonic source or from my own flesh. I can also, as these scriptural accounts and many others show, be engaging in the very structures that witchcraft uses and be walking in righteousness. What does this imply? That there is nothing under the sun that inherently *belongs* to the enemy. We have given him property of God's and of ours as sons and daughters that he never should have had. All things we know as evil are perversions of good, Satan himself being the first example. What if the crux is this:

*What if there is nothing that so belongs to the enemy's camp*
*that I am barred from a redemptive posture*
*and nothing so far inside the camp of God*
*that I am invulnerable to sin?*

Jesus confronted the people of that day this way (in paraphrase): You've heard it said, "Don't commit adultery," but I tell you "Don't even go there in your heart." When Jesus came to complete and fulfill the law, He took it *further* than it had gone before. He called the people to minute-by-minute heart management. No longer could they think they were righteous as long as they tithed 10 percent and observed the Sabbath meticulously. They were now to align with him internally. Much harder work.

*"Little Judy was riding in the car with her father. She decided*
*to stand up in the front seat. Her father commanded her to sit*
*down and put on the seat belt, but she declined. He told her a*
*second time, and again she refused.*

> *"If you don't sit down immediately, I'll pull over to the side of the road and spank you!" Dad finally said, and at this the little girl obeyed. But in a few minutes she said quietly, "Daddy, I'm still standing up inside."*[68]

We want there to be a godly zone and an evil zone of *behavior*, because then we don't have to engage the rigor of constant heart management. But God does not afford us that luxury. The lines just do not fall so clearly in practice. The issue lies within.

Let's expand our look at Numbers 21. The people of Israel had begun to grumble again. They had been rescued from the hands of their Egyptian captors and led by God out into the desert to travel to their promised land. During the journey, when they were without food, God provided miraculously for them. He caused quail to fall to the ground so that they could have meat and caused manna to fall in the mornings like dew. In the midst of these miracles, they grew tired of these provisions and began to complain. The Lord God was so angry with them for their ungratefulness that He sent poisonous snakes among them. Many were bitten and died. They cried out to God to save them. God instructed Moses to *"Make a snake and put it up on a pole; anyone who is bitten can look at it and live." So Moses made a bronze snake and put it up on a pole. Then when anyone was bitten by a snake and looked at the bronze snake, he lived.*[69]

This story includes the forming of a graven image (of a snake, no less), it being lifted up before the people, and healing power coming through gazing upon it. Here, if we looked only at behavior and structures, it would look like idol worship and witchcraft. Why wasn't it? Because by fashioning the snake, Moses was directly obeying God. When the people looked at it and were healed, it was by God's power and choice. The heart's posture of the people was characterized by the acknowledgement of God, repentance, and obedience.

Now some are thinking, "She's promoting 'situational ethics'!" Let's look closely at that, too. If you really look into that philosophy, you'll notice that you're not really bothered by its basic tenet: context defines the morality of a behavior. What bothers you is what secularists have *done* with that simple truth; well it should. They have used it as an excuse to say there *is* no morality—there is no standard for judgment. Once again, the problem is in *conclusion*, not observation.

The fact is that context does in fact define behavior. This is true in both directions. It is also possible to engage in what is normally considered a righteous act and be in sin. Jesus illustrates this point when He condemns the Pharisees for performing all of their righteous acts when their hearts were far from Him. He illustrates it again by saying that there will be those in the last days who do miraculous works and cast out demons "in his name" who will be rejected because He will say to them,

*"I never knew you."*

## The Kicker

Here's the point that brings it all into clarity. The issue "lying within" has nothing to do with whether or not one means well in the popular sense. I am not saying that any sinful act can be defended if someone meant well. It has nothing to do with the Wiccan edict to "only bless". It is not a matter of asking oneself, "Am I a good person?" "Was I trying to help or harm?" The "issue" within is not one of the intention to bless or harm—to do what one understands to be "good" or "evil".

The issue is *Lordship*.

How could God endorse and at times even command so many things in history that seem like witchcraft? Because the problem with witchcraft that makes it so abominable to Him is not a particular practice in and of itself.

It is the *rebellion* and *idolatry* involved. Clearly God does not have a problem with prophecy, dream interpretation, ritual, even divination as long as He is acknowledged and pursued as the one God . . . the only source. He doesn't send Moses into Pharaoh's court with words of condemnation against their witchcraft. *He enables him to outdo them.* It wasn't his acts that distinguished Moses as holy in contrast to their evil. It was his acknowledgement of the I Am—his ambassadorship and obedience. God doesn't say it is abominable to prophesy. He says some of the prophets are *mine* and some are *not*. Some are true and some are false, depending on their *Lord*, their *source*. He doesn't say it is evil to interpret dreams. He says it's evil to interpret them by any means other than HIM! He will have no other gods before Him.

It is similar to the average American Joe Pagan who will tell you that if there turns out to be a Heaven, he'll be going there because he's a "good person". Well, that was never the issue. My standing with God was never about my measure of goodness. It's about whether or not I own Him as Lord. Lordship is the issue. I can be a modern-day Wiccan who loves my fellow man, honors nature, and uses blessing spells to help those in need. For the sake of argument, let's even say that I'm not intentionally calling on any other divine source. I just believe that blessings have inherent positive effect. But Scripture is clear that servitude is not optional. If I am not acknowledging the God of Abraham, Isaac, and Jacob as the Lord and only source, I am at least in rebellion if not overt idolatry. When I pursue special power or knowledge without acknowledging God, *someone* will respond in the supernatural realm. That *someone* will become my lord, whether I know it or not. When you invoke, someone will answer. When you call on the God of Abraham, Isaac, and Jacob, He hears and responds. When you call on anyone else, no matter who you think they are, they will answer as well. And there is no other God beside Him. Either God answers or the enemy does. There is no one else out there. You serve whom you depend upon. Choose this day *whom* you will serve, not if.

We have turned the world on its head. We read accounts like those listed earlier in Scripture that sound like witchcraft. We reason that, "Well, God used those evil things for His good purposes (like a graven image of a snake)." "He is sovereign and He makes the rules," we reason. "He can do that if He chooses. Isn't He great?" But I contend that in reasoning this way we give the enemy far too much credit and that actually the opposite is true. God does not steal something from Satan's camp and use it for good. Everything Satan uses is stolen from *God's* camp and twisted for evil. It all belonged to GOD first. Everything.

*Everything.*

The use of Scripture is a clear example. The atrocities of Hitler, the KKK, and human slavery in the United States were all justified with Scripture. In Matthew 4 we are told that Jesus was led into the desert to be tempted by the enemy. We all know what happens. Satan uses Scripture itself to tempt Jesus. We see him twist and distort those Scriptures to serve his purposes, taking them out of context and using them to appeal to Jesus' weakness. But we would never say in our conservativism, "No, Satan used those Scriptures. They are evil." Of course not. His use of them doesn't make them evil. Neither does his use of the energy system, muscle testing, or intention make them *inherently* evil. It's a theological fallacy to say that anything *belongs* to the enemy and has no redemptive element. The enemy has created nothing. He only distorts.

I remember exactly where I was sitting when this idea hit me. I was astonished by it. I called a trusted friend and said, "You aren't going to believe this." For me it was an arresting thought. Could there really be nothing that *inherently belongs* to the enemy? Do I dare make an argument like that? My mind started running through all the possibilities. What about hatred? Well, God says about Himself that He hates divorce and several other things in Scripture. There is apparently a place for hate within righteousness. What about murder? Well, the act of murder—killing another person—was commanded over and over again by God. What makes it sin to kill another person is the posture of heart, not the act itself. OK, what's the worst thing I can think of . . . child sacrifice? "You mean like God Himself sacrificing His own Son?" my friend replied. Now take a deep breath here. I'm not suggesting we can sacrifice our children in righteousness. I am simply suggesting that everything the enemy does—everything he uses—was stolen from God. The structures used in witchcraft are not effective because they are inherently evil. They are effective because God made them to be. The enemy only warped them for evil use. If combining touch and thought is effective for helping the body resolve trauma, it is not because the enemy made it so, no matter how many people have used it under his authority. It is because God made it so.

Brendan Fraser plays the role in the movie *Blast From the Past* of a young man who has lived his entire life in an underground bunker, raised by parents paralyzed by McCarthy-ist paranoia. He has no framework for the sexual culture that has developed above ground. The movie toys with the contrast. If someone like him were dropped into current sexual culture in America, that person would surely conclude that sexuality is evil. The form it takes in the 21st century is such a dramatic mutation of God's original design that it is hardly recognizable. And yet as a Christian community we don't dare say that sexuality cannot be redeemed. We don't dare conclude that redemption is even the issue, because we know it already belongs to God. The mutation is secondary—not primary. Inherently, sexuality is already holy. The task is not to condemn the creation but to scrape off the mutation. The LORD is *a priori*, not the enemy.

Let's think of it in terms of free will. What if I woke up one day with the startling realization that I can, at any moment, choose to sin? I have this incredible pregnant capacity, waiting spring-loaded, to choose against God. What is He *thinking* giving me that? What an enormous possibility for danger! Well, it's obvious what I must do. I must never decide a single thing again. I must completely divorce myself from this evil potential. That's my only guarantee that I will keep from choosing poorly! In the process of researching for this book, I ran a question by Arthur Burk. He is a prominent Christian teacher with a thorough redemptive posture. I asked him, "What do you think is the difference between witchcraft and Christian, authoritative prayer? They are each attempting to alter things somehow." He said that he doesn't think there is a clear line. I didn't like that answer, but he's right in one sense. There is not a clear line in practice, but there is a clear line in Lordship. Can we draw a line down the middle of free will? Can we say, "These acts are sin, and these are holy?" Not definitively, no, because as the story of the bronze snake shows us, heart's posture defines behavior. I do not deny my capacity to choose because of its potential for evil. I fight for holiness. I fight in every moment for the right to say "Whatever I do, I do it unto the Lord." We are given so many warnings in Scripture of the destructive power of the tongue. Do we cease to speak? Of course not. We walk the line, knowing that I can speak both within the will of God and outside of it.

If my cousin sat me down at that table again today, I would respond differently. We both looked at that imaginary marker she drew and assumed together that we had a shared definition of "the line". But did we? I'm not nearly as sure now that there is a clear line in practice. The line is in the heart; the heart's management is dynamic, fluid, and requires constant watch and transparency to the Spirit of God.

On the one hand, this seems like a wildly liberal argument. But on the other hand, it is ultimately conservative because there is no get-out-of-jail-free card. Whether I eat or drink or whatever I do, I am to do it unto the Lord. That can be as difficult on the mission field as it is at yoga class. Recognizing that the issue lies within does not make things easier. It makes them harder. It does not relieve me from the strenuous work of holiness. It intensifies it. Watching over my heart is difficult. It would be much easier if I could just tithe 10 percent, stay faithful to my spouse, go to church every Sunday, and never have to look at my heart.

So, could you be doing the "intention and circuitry" of Energy Psychology and be doing witchcraft? Of course you could. If you understand the "energy" you're manipulating to be the universal "god" force and have no acknowledgement or pursuit of the LORD as the creator of that mechanism in the body, then you are probably doing witchcraft. By His natural design we influence with our touch and intention, but I can do that "unto Him" or not. I can do it in obedience to Him or in rebellion. So as we established earlier, the seemingly subtle shift into the pursuit/manipulation of energy *as god* ruins the whole endeavor.

## In the Garden

In the garden God gives us overwhelming authority to reign with Him. He gives His creatures astounding elevation—wild license. "Populate! *Name* everything even! Go nuts!" And in the center of this riotous adventure he places the Tree—the Tree of the Knowledge of Good and Evil. Some biblical commentators have noted that Genesis may be using a common figure of speech in that passage. They suggest that "*the knowledge of good and evil*" may have been used figuratively in Hebrew like we would say "From A to Z". If so, it might have been translated "The Tree of the Knowledge of All Things". Either way, God is saying that "in the midst of the grand honor of reigning with Me, I will present before you a continual choice. I will cause you to have to choose by your obedience or disobedience around that tree, continually . . . who gets to have all the knowledge. You get to choose every day to let *Me* be the one who knows all things . . . who is sovereign over the future and all things I have chosen to make hidden. Reign liberally with Me here on this lovely earth I've given you . . . fill the earth, subdue it . . . go nuts . . . and decide every day, within all the incredible authority I've given you to co-reign with Me . . .

decide every day anew, to *let Me be God* . . . when you have the option in front of you (or so I let you think) of taking it for yourself. Surrender by choice."

A stunning invitation to intimacy, but we turned Him down. We chose to take godhood for ourselves. And ever since then the battle rages on as we try every way under heaven to eat that fruit . . . to have all power and all knowledge by any means we can, instead of letting Him be God. He says, "If you want to know, ask *Me*. If you need power . . . consult *Me*. I have offered you my Spirit . . . the very Spirit that raised Jesus from the dead!"

## One Without the Other

There is a useful distinction to make here between the acts of witchcraft and its heart posture, because I can easily have one without the other and still be on dangerous ground. The specific structures employed by witchcraft have been named earlier (for the most part). We have already established that many of the specific structures employed by witchcraft are counterfeits of God's own structures that He used in working with His people. Nevertheless, one can engage in one of those act/structures which the enemy has tried to claim and be honoring—even obeying—God. Scripture gives us multiple examples of this. Similarly, I can be engaged in what would typically be thought of as a godly act/structure and be very much in the heart posture of witchcraft . . . the pursuit of special power or knowledge.

If God so repeatedly tells His people that witchcraft is abominable, then why does He use so many of the same structures commonly employed in witchcraft? He uses those structures because they are originally *His*. He is the one who built it into natural law that ritual, for instance, is useful to focus us in *His* presence. It is *His* design that words are constitutive, *His* design that the oils and herbs in nature impact us, *His* desire that we would have means to consult Him and receive a response. The enemy uses these structures precisely *because they are effective*. Those structures misused by witchcraft are *supposed* to invoke . . . to invoke Him. They naturally call upon that which is more than ourselves . . . *super*natural. If I want special knowledge or power, its very definition as "special" means that it cannot come from man or the natural order. It is supernatural. But it was never God's intention that we would be divorced from the supernatural . . . only that we would know it only as Him. Whether I intend to be pursuing a supernatural sentience or not, the structures on witchcraft naturally do so. That was God's idea, not Satan's.

Now what if I used one of the structures semi-neutrally? What if I engaged in a structure of witchcraft without meaning at all to utilize supernatural power? What if I just thought the structures had inherent effect? Let's look at it this way:

If I am speaking what I believe to be a spell, for instance, and in my heart I have no thought of demonic entities—no desire to connect with any personhood per se, and I'm only looking to bless a friend, the intention of a spell (i.e. words believed to be supernaturally empowered) *does invoke*, whether I like it or not. God Himself made it to. Invocation is not the issue. Invocation is natural. "Come, Lord Jesus!" is invocation. Every foxhole prayer is invocation. The issue is *whom* you invoke. And who is lord of whom. When the witch invokes the goddess of nature, she assumes that as long as she follows the prescribed incantation or steps of ritual, the goddess is bound to her wishes— obligated to carry out her demands. She is acting as lord.

Aren't we vulnerable to this type of witchcraft as well? Rarely would we overtly articulate it this way, but we often live as if God owes us certain things because we've obeyed Him or served Him to exhaustion or denied the flesh for Him. We become indignant at His blatant lack of obligation to us. There are even books like *Bible Spells* by William Alexander Oribello and *Powers of the Psalms* by Anna Riva that teach the reader how to use psalms and various other Scriptures to gain power and knowledge—to force God to make good on His debt to us.

I asked my client about her little finger. It was bent to the side and difficult to use. I was curious about how it had happened. She began to tell me that years earlier she was painting her basement and fell off of a ladder and broke her pinky. But before she could finish the story, she stopped herself, visibly frustrated with her own thoughtlessness. She said, "No. No. In the Name of Jesus, this pinky is healed!" I contend that that is not faith. Her pinky was not healed. The tired mantra "Name it and claim it" is a Christian version of "the gods are obligated."

Lordship is the issue.

CHAPTER 10

# What is Splankna Therapy?

*"Few things are harder to put up with than a good example."*
*—Mark Twain*

B y now we have established several definitions. We've defined *Energy, Energy Psychology, New Age,* and *Witchcraft.* Next I will give you a detailed look into the Splankna Protocol so that in the next chapter we can evaluate it through these lenses.

As I have said, I never intended to be this person. I would never have dreamed up this career. Needless to say I never intended to teach it to anyone else either. Directing a training institute for Christian therapists and healthcare providers was not my plan. But when we give our days to God, He will do what He will. Over the years of wading with Him through these waters a unique mind-body protocol morphed into existence. I found that He and I had designed an Energy Psychology protocol based on a biblical foundation. Here we'll walk through a detailed description of a Splankna session.

## "Splankna"? (splawnk-nuh)

I'm sure you've been wondering about the origin of the name. During my undergraduate work in the Bible department I had to take a semester of Greek under Dr. Tom Geer. I'm one of those students who can memorize really quickly and easily, but I won't remember it tomorrow. So unfortunately, most of my Greek swiftly left my head. I still remember some of the more commonly known terms such as *ecclesia* (called out ones) and *hamartia* (sin), but it's pretty sparing. For some reason, one of the only other Greek words that stuck with me was *splankna*. Dr. Geer extrapolated one day explaining that while the term is literally translated *bowels* or *guts* (lovely), it was used socio-culturally at the time the way we use the word *subconscious*—as if to say "I know it in my gut." I always thought it was strange that I remembered that. But when it came time to name the protocol, it was clear. It's the worst possible name from a promotional standpoint. It's so clumsy and odd. I love it.

## How Does It Look?

The Splankna Therapy protocol aims at handling the emotional, physical, and spiritual fuel behind psychological symptoms at the same time so that they are thoroughly relieved with the least probability of recidivism. I'll describe an average Splankna session in somewhat of a narrative form. We'll call our Splankna practitioner John and our client Erin.

Erin is a devoted Christian who has suffered all of her life with an acute fear of heights. (For this illustration we will use the earlier-mentioned example of a childhood fall translating into a fear of heights.) She has made an appointment with John based on a trusted referral. When she arrives for her first session, John greets her and has her fill out a client intake packet. This includes a disclosure statement for confidentiality, a description of John's credentials, a brief explanation of the protocol, and a questionnaire that helps John understand her history and symptoms. John will first listen to Erin's story. He will ask about her family history, the history of the symptom, her conclusions about the symptom's origin, and her goals for their work.

### Prayer

When all the information is gathered, they pray together to open the session. They present Erin's heart's desires before the Lord, but they also invite God to override that if His own priorities are different. Often God will prefer to work on other things before He addresses the symptom that the client is bringing up. The two most common trumping priorities of His seem to be significant relational blocks between Him and the client or a gift and call issue. If the client wants to clear an addiction but has always had a deep fear of the wrath of God, for instance, He may begin with the fear and then address the addiction. The other thing that tops His priority list is the client being significantly out of line with His call on that person's life. It often seems more important to Him to that I am fulfilling my role in the larger story than whether or not I fight with this or that symptom.

In prayer John and Erin lay themselves out before the Lord. Everything past, present, and future—soul, spirit, and body. They ask the Lord Jesus to gather up any warfare that applies to either one of them and seal it under His feet during their work. They ask that He would rise up intercession for them if they need it. They ask the Lord to take hold of their will and align it with His. As we discussed earlier, the deep heart/subconscious is fear-based and resistant. Every seat of the will is given to the Lord, asking Him to align their will with His own. They ask that God would supply to them the necessary faith, strength, courage, and wisdom to follow where He leads. Then they invite the Holy Spirit to search through Erin's heart and choose the place where He would like to begin (Prov. 20:27). They thank

Him ahead of time for what He will do. They work under the assumption that if we hand ourselves over to the Lord and invite Him to move on our hearts, He will take us up on that. Of course each practitioner has his or her own style in prayer, but these are the typical basics.

When the prayer is complete, John trusts that the Holy Spirit did indeed search through the database of Erin's heart and choose a place to begin. John assumes that her heart and body have awareness of this move. He now uses a muscle test to "ask" her system (spirit/soul/body) where in her heart's record did the Spirit choose? He is not using the muscle test to ask God but to ask Erin's own system what spot in the heart God just pointed out. This is an important distinction. Using a muscle test as a voice-piece for God is dishonoring. He is not a jukebox of answers waiting for my command. On the contrary, John and Erin give God all sovereignty in the process. They will go and work only where He chooses.

## Clearing Traumatic Emotions

So now they are ready to work. John has two 8.5 x 11 charts. One is Splankna's Emotion Chart. This has been adapted from Scott Walker's work in Neuro-Emotional Technique. The idea here, as we discussed in Chapter 3, is that the body seems to store emotions and memory on a physiological/energetic level. There is organization to that storage. The body's 14 Energy Meridians each store particular flavors of emotion. For instance, rage would be stored in a Liver Meridian and betrayal in a Lung Meridian. The chart lists the different types of emotions and where they are stored in the body. John will use the chart to help Erin's heart navigate her reaction to the trauma. The Emotion Chart cannot contain every possible human emotion, but it covers the gamut well enough to enable her to process her experience. John's other chart is his Protocol Chart. It is a pictorial decision tree that walks him through the steps of the work.

Most of the time, the work takes the form of what Splankna calls a "Set", so we will use that as our example for John and Erin. A Set consists of the trauma emotions that were stored in the body from a particular moment in Erin's history and the Agreement made with the enemy around that trauma. We will get to agreement in a moment. First let's walk through the trauma emotions with John and Erin.

John has Erin hold her arm out in front of her. She stiffens her deltoid muscle moderately to give him some resistance. When he asks about an age or an emotion that is off the mark (with which her system is not congruent) and applies pressure to her wrist, nothing occurs. Her arm remains strong. When he asks about an age or an emotion with which her system *is* congruent, it creates a minor reaction in her energy system. That energetic shift affects the strengthened muscle and does something like de-activate it; instead of holding strong, Erin's muscle gently gives way. We described in Chapter 2 that on the energetic level, thought seems to have some kind of signature resonance or frequency. Erin's body is thought to be responding to that frequency of the meaning that John is sending.

John first asks for the age of the trauma they are dealing with. He ascertains the age by testing through a simple process of elimination, e.g. "Did this trauma occur between your conception and birth, from your birth to age 5, from 5 to 10 years old, from 10 to 15?" and so forth. John then asks about the "central emotion". There may be anywhere from two to 12 trauma emotions that Erin has stored from this memory. John wants to know what her heart considers to be the main theme of them all. This helps inform him for future steps. He uses the Emotion Chart to pinpoint the central emotion in the Set. He asks which Meridian it is stored in and then which specific emotion in that list.

When Erin's muscle has responded to a particular age for this trauma and a particular central emotion, John has her employ Energy Psychology's change agent: circuitry + intention. She simply touches a point on her body that is along the particular Meridian while thinking about that emotion/trauma. Let's say John gets a weak muscle response when he hits the age of 8 in Erin's history. He then goes through the emotion chart and gets a weak muscle response when he names the emotion of fear. He then asks her if she is aware of a fearful trauma at that age. She may or may not be aware of anything in particular. If she does remember the trauma, he will have her think about feeling fear during that trauma as she holds the Meridian point on her body. If she does not remember a relevant trauma, he will have her hold the point and just imagine feeling intense fear at that age. For our example we'll say she does remember the trauma. She tells John the story of falling out of a tree and breaking her arm. The bone was protruding from her skin. Her mother panicked and called an ambulance. She remembers being terrified by all of the sirens and commotion and especially by her mother's panic.

John then has her think about that trauma while she holds the Meridian point that accesses the stored emotion of fear. When she has held the circuitry + intention for a few seconds, he tests her arm to see if the emotion "cleared" physiologically. This is where some of that previously mentioned mystery comes into play. The body seems to be able to resolve or release Erin's stored emotion on an energetic level. Her memory of the trauma does not change, but the combination of touch and thought somehow detaches the memory from the emotion. No one in psychology or science is exactly sure yet how that happens, but reliably it does.

## Forgiveness

If the emotion tests as cleared, John moves on. He asks how many emotions there are total in this Set and then tests for the next one following the same pattern. But any time an emotion does not test as cleared through the simple touch and thought, John moves Erin into forgiveness work. Forgiveness is essential for healing (1 John 1:9, Mt. 6:14). A heart held in bitterness cannot be restored. We are instructed to forgive one another throughout Scripture (Eph. 4:23, Col. 3:13); it is considered an integral part of the Splankna Protocol.

John and Erin are working on the third emotion of seven that were stored from Erin's traumatic fall. The first two emotions were "fear" (stored in the Kidney Meridian) and "powerlessness" (stored in the Liver Meridian). The third emotion is "dread". John is not clear about how dread applies to this trauma, so he asks Erin about it. "In what way do you think you would have felt dread during that trauma?" Erin brings up her mother. She describes that her mother's reaction made her feel like it must be the end of the world. She wondered if she was going to die. John then has her think about that specific dread while touching her Kidney Meridian point. He then tests, but the emotion has not cleared. This indicates that in order to finish the resolution of that emotion, Erin needs to forgive.

In this context it is fairly obvious to John that she might need to forgive her mother. He has her tap softly on the side of her little finger (fingertip points seem to correlate to forgiveness. This correlation was drawn from Dr. Callahan's work). As she taps, he has her speak out loud, "I forgive my mother for her reaction to that trauma", or "I forgive my mother for making me afraid I was going to die." John then re-tests to see if the emotion is cleared. If it is, he moves on to the next one in this Set of seven. If it is not cleared, he tries another forgiveness statement toward her mother or checks to see if there is anyone else whom Erin needs to forgive. When forgiveness is complete, the emotion will test as cleared. Forgiveness can be the most difficult part of the process. At times a client might feel that they are unable or unwilling to forgive. If Erin expressed that kind of difficulty, John would encourage her to speak it out loud anyway and trust that by speaking it, she helps her heart move in that direction.

Through this format, John and Erin clear the trauma emotions that she stored physiologically from that childhood experience. This work has moved both body and soul toward healing. Now it is time for them to address Erin's spirit.

## Agreement

There is also a spiritual component to the trauma. There are many legitimate ways to handle the enemy's role in our lives. The framework that God has led Splankna to use is the metaphor of "Agreement". We think of it something like this: in our moments of emotional intensity, whether in the form of anger, pain, fear, etc., the enemy capitalizes on our vulnerability by offering deals to the deep heart . . . coping strategies, exchanges. When we agree with one of these offerings, we make an Agreement with the enemy. It is reminiscent of the way he tempted Jesus in the desert. When God came to earth and took on flesh, Satan was given one official shot at tempting him. Of all the possible styles of temptation, Satan used bargaining. He poked at what he thought would be Jesus' vulnerable areas and offered Him deals. "You give me this; I'll give you that." It's as if something like that happens in our lives as well. The enemy tries to get us to bargain with him to resolve our traumas.

It is a legal universe. Everything that goes on in the spirit realm is ordered. All things follow God's laws of right and authority. There are rules. When Satan wanted to torment Job and prove that he only loved God because of blessing, he had to ask God's permission. At the Cross, the enemy lost inherent right to mankind through the sacrifice and resurrection of Jesus. We came out from under the law of sin and death (Rom. 8:2). Subsequently, Satan and his camp attempt to gain back some right to our lives in different ways. Again, I don't know how literally this happens, but at least symbolically, the enemy seems to show up in our traumatic moments and offer coping strategies or guarantees, for example. If somewhere in the deep heart I agree, then I give them a degree of right/access to me.

We agree with these offerings because we are deceived into believing that they are necessary. We get deceived into believing that a particular bargain with warfare will serve some needed purpose. The result is that these Agreements are another kind of the fuel behind our symptoms. I cannot say with certainty that we literally make "deals with the devil" but just that it is a way of thinking about things that is close enough to reality that it gets the job done. I *am* confident that it is the framework God has led me to use in this protocol and that He works within it powerfully.

So John and Erin have cleared out the trauma emotions that she has been carrying from her 8-year-old trauma. It is assumed that those emotions have been causing or fueling her fear of heights. Whenever she experiences height (or possibly even when she thinks about height), all of her natural associations kick in. Her system says to itself, "What do we have stored about height? What framework have I built to interpret height?" It taps her "height file"; up comes her stored traumatic emotions. With Splankna, she has just resolved those emotions physiologically; they are no longer stored in her file. Those emotions are no longer associated with height in her system. They could stop here and she would most likely have nice results. However, if they continue on and deal with any possible warfare element, they will be more thorough. They want to handle all possible sources of fuel behind this symptom, so they continue.

Erin's trauma emotions are cleared, and it is time to deal with any possible Agreement with the enemy that she may have made around the event. The Agreement is considered to be another kind of fuel behind her symptom (fear of heights). Metaphorically, we think of the Agreement as being rooted in the subconscious. The conscious mind operates like the "spirit man" (Rom. 7) and does not generally agree with symptoms, but something deep within me does. I want to be careful in pointing out that Splankna does not assume that all symptoms are a direct result of Agreement. Symptoms can exist without the involvement of Agreement. I am not saying that we have all agreed with the enemy for every negative thing we experience or even for every emotional or physical symptom we struggle with. I'm simply saying that it is useful to break any Agreements that are related regardless of other ontological elements.

During the development of this protocol, the concept of Agreement has morphed a few times. For several years before I considered teaching this to anyone else, the possible styles of Agreement became a bit exhaustive. When it came time to formulate the protocol into teachable format, I knew I had to simplify things. As always I asked the Lord for guidance and narrowed it down to five styles of Agreement. Again, these are only metaphorical frameworks to assist the heart in removing any enemy influence in a trauma and the symptoms it spawned. The five styles of Agreement used in the Splankna Protocol are as follows: Ownership, Program, Power, Transfer, and Assault Agreements. A thorough explanation of these is beyond the scope of this book and would make it feel like a manual. So in order to continue our narrative, we'll just look closely into one of them.

Let's get back to John and Erin and watch this playing out. John asks which of the styles of Agreement they are working with. "Program Agreement" tests congruent. In this context, John reasons that Erin may have agreed to an emotional program of "fear of heights". The reasoning here is that when the trauma occurred and Erin was vulnerable and overwhelmed with emotion, the enemy capitalized on the moment by offering her a coping strategy and a guarantee for the future. If she agreed to the fear of heights, she can be assured that this sort of trauma will never befall her again. A phobia masquerades as a protective mechanism. If I phobically avoid "A", then "A" will never happen. When I agree with this offering from the enemy, I give the right to operate this phobia in my system. If the trauma emotions were cleared but the Agreement was not broken, the improvement would not be as complete or as permanent.

John and Erin return now to prayer. Agreements are broken following the basic steps lined out for us in Scripture. John walks Erin through confession and repentance. She confesses that somewhere in her heart there has been Agreement with the fear of heights. She repents of that Agreement and all of the impact it has had on her life and her relationship with God. Following these biblical steps affords Erin the full right to break the Agreement on behalf of all of her system, by the authority of Jesus, so Erin now revokes the Agreement. Now that the Agreement is broken, they do a little housekeeping. In Jesus' Name they command all demonic entities that were associated with the Agreement to leave. Some send demons to the Abyss. I've only felt led to send them to the feet of Jesus, where He can do with them what He pleases. By the authority of Jesus, John and Erin pray for the reversal of the effects of the Agreement. They ask the Lord Jesus to breathe His life into the affected areas and reign there from then on. Following the prompting of the Spirit, they continue to pray for any issues of repair and restoration that apply. They thank the Lord for what He has done.

The Set is now complete. Most of the time, that is a pretty close approximation of a Splankna Therapy session. There are some variations, but that is a good summation. Not all of the work takes the form of a Set, but it accounts for approximately 75 percent. Some symptoms are one-dimensional; some are complicated and multi-layered. The fruit of the work will show during the ensuing days and weeks. John and Erin will both take note of her progress and continue to bring her requests before the Lord as needed.

While a Set is done most of the time, other times during a Splankna session, Algorithm work is done. The client will focus on the trauma or symptom while tapping through a sequence of Meridian points on the head and torso. The useful order of these tapping points was developed by Dr. Callahan, but when they reach the point where he would do the 9g sequence (counting, looking down right and left, etc.) they interject bilateral eye movements instead (synthesized from E.M.D.R.—Chapter 3).

Bilateral stimulation usually takes the form of eye movements. The practitioner holds two fingers in front of the client and moves them back and forth quickly while the client tracks visually. For some reason, this back and forth movement helps to "unstick" the brain. Algorithms and bilateral stimulation assist the body and brain in finishing out partially processed trauma. When the brain attempts to process a trauma, it can get overloaded and stuck, like a skipping CD. Algorithms and bilateral stimulation are most useful in assisting the brain/body get past that point and complete resolution. This type of work is usually interjected as a smaller piece of the whole, rather than being used alone. The practitioner's protocol chart allows him to navigate which steps to use in session and when.

It's important to mention here that the Splankna protocol is not a panacea. Nothing is. It does not hit the mark every time. For instance, we can take 10 people with a fear of spiders or a smoking addiction or clinical depression and walk them through the same protocol. Eight out of 10 will have wonderful results. Their symptoms will lift permanently. But two of them will not respond; we do not know exactly why. This relates to why Energy Psychology does not lend itself well to typical research designs. There is more at play than we understand. My husband has reminded me *ad nauseam* that, "This might work for different reasons than we think." I hope this gave you an overall feel for the work. Mystery and limits admitted, it still amazes me every day to see what God does with this tool. I feel deeply privileged to have been a part of it. Watching God work through this protocol has been such an adventure. It has taught me so much about His nature. I am truly grateful.

# CHAPTER 11

# The Redemptive Thinker

*"Honest disagreement is often a good sign of progress."*
*—Mahatma Gandhi*

S o how would an informed Christian navigate the world of energy healing from a biblically redemptive posture? Now that you've walked through a Splankna session, we will use it as our example. Let's evaluate the protocol through the lenses of New Age and witchcraft.

## The Rubber and The Road

The two elements (structures) used in our style of Energy Psychology are these:

muscle testing
circuitry + intention.

These two are used in the identifying and clearing of a stored trauma emotion. That first day when I left Dr. Martin's office, my instant question was, "How is a muscle test any different than a Ouija board or a crystal ball?" This is a very important question. Ouija boards and crystal balls and all other forms of divination have both of our witchcraft definitions in common.

They intend to pursue *special knowledge* through *special power*.

How do these practices manage to cross both boundaries at once? *They are typically meant to be utilized by a third party.* They are meant to be voice boxes for third party, sentient responses. The assumption is that some supernatural conscious source responds to a question asked *through* the object because that supernatural source knows the answer. That source has the special knowledge; the object will create the necessary bridge between the entity and the user. It is assumed that some otherworldly source of knowledge causes the tarot card to rise to the top of the stack and the tea leaves to form their meaningful pattern, etc. The obvious accusation is that muscle testing is doing the same thing. But let's look closely.

## Muscle Testing

The way that muscle testing is used within the Splankna protocol, it actually contains neither of those characteristics. While a muscle test certainly can be used to pursue special knowledge or power, it does not do so *inherently*.

The first crucial difference in Spankna's use of muscle testing is *the absence of third party involvement.* (This could apply of course to any other Christian practice of muscle testing.) When a muscle responds in congruence or incongruence to an idea, it is my own body's reaction, like sprouting a rash when I come into contact with an allergen. No spiritual entity is speaking through the muscle test or causing it to react. The body naturally displays its own congruence and incongruence through many means. The fact that a muscle will respond to an energetic/electrical shift that goes off in the body is just a part of God's unsearchable design. It is not empowered by the enemy. How do I know? Most pointedly because a person's system (believer or not) has awareness of demonic influence. Any type of demonic influence or activity that has affected the person is catalogued in the body and subconscious, just like all other experiences. Reliably, the body can express this awareness through a muscle test, allowing the demonic element to be exposed and removed in prayer. If the enemy inherently controlled muscle testing, we wouldn't be able to use it to expose him and cast him off. A house divided against itself would fall (Luke 11:17).

Secondly, we need to further define the *special* in special knowledge. The information that muscle testing is accessing in the Splankna protocol is not special. It is the heart and body's own data. The only information we can legitimately test for is the client's own record of their trauma emotions, their own memories, their own reactions, and adopted coping strategies. We are meticulous about this boundary line. My own stored emotions are mine to search. They are not "special". Any time a muscle test is used to access information not within the person and about the person, the line is crossed into witchcraft. For instance, although my client has awareness about her husband's emotions, it is out of boundaries to test her body about his data. That is special knowledge. It is also outside of boundaries to test for future knowledge or judgment questions. Any question that starts with "Should I . . .?" is out of line. The subconscious is not my leader. I do not have all wisdom on any level. Questions that involve making a choice (judgment) do not belong in a muscle test.

This takes us back to the discussion of constant heart management. Sometimes the boundaries can be difficult to discern. For instance, muscle testing is used in many Christian holistic circles for nutritional purposes. A nutritionist might ask a client to hold a vitamin in their hand and muscle test for the body's reaction to that substance . . . does my body respond like it wants that or rejects that? This is a fair question. It is a nutritional example of my body's own data. Again, it is similar to placing an allergic substance on my skin and seeing my body's reaction to it. However, when I ask, "Will I ever get breast cancer like my mother did?", I've crossed over into future telling and witchcraft.

## Reiki as An Example

Now, for greater clarity, let's evaluate another energy healing protocol through this same lens. Let's look at Reiki, for example. Reiki is an energetic, mind-body treatment protocol in the same genre. Generally the Reiki practitioner learns to move and re-align the patient's physical energy system through another means. They either touch the patient's body or hold the hands several inches above the body (typically) and learn to physically feel the body's subtle energy system. They learn to feel with their hands the flow and blockages of a person's body energy and can supposedly move it gently back into order and balance through focused intention and the movement of their hands.

Originally, orthodox Reiki taught its practitioners that the way to develop this sensitivity was to access a "spirit guide". This is thought to be because the originator of Reiki, Mikao Usui, was raised in Japanese Shintoism with its focus on divine spirits in nature. Throughout Reiki treatment, one's spirit guide intimately directs the process. These entities are understood by New Age practitioners to be positive supernatural beings such as angels or the spirits of gifted healers of the past.[70] There has been some speculation that Usui was a Christian, but it has not been verified. Even if he was, the philosophy and practice of Reiki since his death has not developed within a Christian worldview.

Thankfully there are many training institutions where one can learn the basic principles of Reiki without the use of spirit guides. Many Christians have done so. But when there *is* the use of a spirit guide, we have obvious third party involvement that is not God. We have had many non-Christian Reiki practitioners contend that our prayer for the leadership of the Holy Spirit is no different than their practice with spirit guides. But there is a crucial difference. First of all, as we have already established, if you are not clear about who God is when you call on the supernatural, someone else will answer. God does not offer us spirit guides. He has his angels who obey Him and assist us, but they are not at our command like a genie in a bottle. But the Reiki practitioner's use of their spirit guide is akin to the Wiccan's use of the goddess. That entity is obligated—bound to the invocation and will of the practitioner. Regardless of how powerfully the Spirit of the Living God may move through me in any given moment, He never offers me the right or power to invoke Him at will to do my bidding.

This is one of the rules of thumb when it comes to questionable spiritual "gifting". Occasionally, clients will have some special ability that is in question. They are not sure if it is from God. One of the easiest tests is Lordship. Can you turn that "gift" on and off at will? Is it at your discretion? If so, it may not be of God.

Agnes Sanford, author of *The Healing Light* and many other books, recounts what it was like to operate in a profound spiritual gift of physical healing. It was commonplace for her to lay her hands on a broken knee and feel it move under the skin. She saw terminal illnesses disappear and twisted legs walk. But even she knew that God's power was not at her discretion. Whenever she was asked to pray for someone's healing, she would ask the Lord about it. She explains that sometimes He would say, "No, I do not have healing for them through your prayers. Just sit with them."[71]

## The Authority of Touch

Reiki brings up another interesting point because it is sometimes administered without touching the client. God has built great order into His creation; He seems to have given touch a unique measure of authority. We are familiar, of course, with Jesus' practice of touching those He healed and with our scriptural instructions to lay on hands in prayer. God has built something special into touch.

The common understanding in the secular energy world was that there is something like what Carl Jung coined "universal consciousness". It is theorized in the New Age/energy world that on the subconscious level, we all know everything. Literally. The thought process goes something like this: since emotions and thoughts have an energetic frequency that emanates out of us, we all subconsciously read this off of one another around the globe. Theoretically, I know everything about you and could muscle test it if I wanted to. Hopefully it is unnecessary for me to go into the myriad of theological and ethical problems with that kind of practice. But based on this theory and the trust that a muscle test is part of God's natural processes, many Christians practice what we call "remote testing", as long as they have the permission of the tested individual. This is any form of testing without touch (i.e. testing over the phone).

Throughout the years, I have always felt a "yellow light" about remote testing. I believe that there is a God-given authority endorsement in touch. I am convinced that although the information probably is there in the quantum field between us, it is one step out of bounds to access it without touch. It is possible, in my opinion, that when a believer employs the practice of remote testing, he becomes like the Wicca who doesn't intend to draw in demonic involvement through the incantation but unwittingly may. If this is so, it would be because accessing the information without touch renders that information special because it is really the tester's own body responding—similar to testing my client's body for information about her husband.

It is of course plausible that God could teach someone the kind of sensitivity and understanding needed to help balance and align someone's Meridian energy even without touch if He chose to. I believe He could use that for His purposes just like anything else. And as we've mentioned, more modern Reiki training does not always involve the use of spirit guides. I also believe that the vulnerability created (if I am correct) by the lack of touch in remote testing can be covered and protected by His grace if an obedient believer was seeking and acknowledging Him as Lord. But so far, I remain under conviction that touch matters and that it's *better* to honor it. If the lack of touch renders the information *special*, I'd err on the conservative. I do not pretend to be the ultimate authority on these issues; I know I could be wrong. I may find, 10 years from now, that this stance was too conservative, but up until this point it is still my best understanding.

## Circuitry + Intention

The other main structure we're using is "circuitry + intention." Why isn't this witchcraft? As we've already discussed, as Newtonian physics suggested that the universe is one big machine, quantum physics suggests the Logos. All things are sustained by His powerful Word. God maintains the universe, animates it, intervenes in it, and keeps the particles buzzing by His *will*. He intends it to and it does. And He has given us the immeasurable honor of also bearing, in reflective, diminutive measure, constitutive intention. Our will affects reality, not in sovereignty but in reflection of *imago dei*. It is part of being a human and not a rock.

We are constantly reigning with God in or outside of obedience whether we know it or not. He allows us constant input. In the "touch and thought" of Energy Psychology we are just being purposeful about it. There is no necessity for a third party to supernaturally assist us. It is our inherent privilege and responsibility. It was God's idea for touch to be impactful, as we have already established. For the Meridian system to give us a little detail behind that injunction is just like any other part of science ... our continued discovery of his unsearchable creation and its wonders. Far from undermining Him, it declares His works. And it is God who gets the glory for the effect of circuitry and intention, not any other source, even His creation itself.

## A Measuring Stick

Our whole argument boils down to this: The lines of righteousness cannot be easily drawn in behavior. They are drawn in the heart—in Lordship. What makes New Age and witchcraft (and any other practice) abominable to God is the rebellion and idolatry within them. For the Christian, any healing protocol must pass these tests:

1. *Does it deny the hierarchy and personhood of God?*

2. *Does it pursue special knowledge or special power?*

3. *Does it invoke anyone or anything other than God himself?*

Let's put acupuncture through this test. Basically, acupuncture attempts to rebalance the flow of the body's energy system through the insertion of needles along Meridian lines. They are thought to act like little antennae – redrawing the energy current into areas where it is weak or has been blocked. Does this practice deny the hierarchy and personhood of God? Not inherently. The theory and practice of acupuncture are not spiritual or moral in and of themselves. The issue lies with the practitioner. What if my acupuncturist believes in Chinese healing gods? What if his intention is to bring them into his work? What if he relies on their intervention for the client's healing? Then as a practitioner, he is invoking someone other than the God of the Bible.

But what if my practitioner is an agnostic? What if he was trained in acupuncture from a Westernized institution for alternative medicine and sees his work as purely physical? In this case, his work can pass the three tests. Obviously it would be even more beneficial if he understands that it is God who created the amazing Meridian System of Energy and he bathes his work in prayer, but God's designs work, whether or not we acknowledge him as their source.

Several years ago I read one of the books in the popular self-help series *Men Are from Mars and Women Are from Venus*. It was recommended by my soon-to-be husband the first time he asked me out. It was *Mars and Venus On A Date*. I was surprised to find that the secular author, John Gray was promoting God's design. I found it really amusing though that he thought it was his own invention. He describes in the book how attraction between men and women happens. He explains that if a man does the pursuing and a woman does the responding, everything works. Genius! He takes the reader through each stage of a romantic relationship, applying his convention. He shows how attraction grows as long as the prescription is followed and diminishes when it is not. But there is one chapter where he changes his tune. He describes in its introduction that the formula seems to break down at this stage in the romantic development; he's not sure why. What is this stage? Sexual intimacy before marriage, of course. Whether or not you acknowledge them as His, God's designs work. An unbeliever can work within general truth.

Let's consider a third scenario. What if my acupuncturist professes to be a Christian but upon further discussion reveals that he is embracing not only of Christianity but of all religions as expressions of truth? What if he is a professing Christian who invokes a spirit guide or the advice of a dead loved one? In these cases, the lines are crossed. The question is not "Is the practitioner a professing Christian?" Professing Christianity does not make it acceptable to cross into idolatry or rebellion. These are heart's postures of sin wherever they are found.

## Eating Meat in The 21st Century

Scripture tells us that *to the pure, all things are pure* (Titus 1:15). It does not say, "To the pure, all things are dangerous." Scripture assumes that greater purity in Christ means greater redemptive freedom. The apostle Paul's discussion on eating meat is relevant here. In 1 Corinthians Paul is addressing a divisive issue in the church. The culture surrounding them regularly offered its meat as a sacrifice to idols before selling it in the marketplace. The believers were torn over how to respond to this. Some of them had just come to Christ from that very culture. They probably spent most of their lives worshiping those idols. It was a dramatic internal shift for them to decide that what they had always worshiped was false and empty. For them, to eat meat sacrificed to idols was all too familiar. They were unable to separate that practice from the heart's posture of idol worship.

To others who had never given credit to the idols, the issue seemed trivial. They knew very well that the idols were empty and that the meat belonged to God. It was no problem for them to disregard the dedication as well, considering it empty. In its historical context, this "disputable" issue would not have seemed trivial. To the weak it was a great danger and to the strong a proud freedom. Their culture believed and intended to give that meat over to demon gods. That is significant. Demonic entities back up those idols and the entity receives the dedication. A dedication isn't void. It is substantive in the spirit realm. And yet, even in that context, Paul defines it as a matter of maturity. He says it would only be those weaker in faith who wouldn't be able to maintain a redemptive posture—who would not be able to steal back what was God's creation (meat) and clean off the demonic intention ascribed to it.

He is saying that if you are a "weaker brother" and to you, eating meat that's been sacrificed to idols is engaging in your old occultic/pre-Christian practices, then to you it is sin and you should not do it. But clearly your emotional position is the point. If a person believes something to be sin and does it anyway, to that person it is sin. Paul is saying it's only unredeemable if that's what you believe about it . . . how you associate it. The stronger brother can easily redeem it. Paul makes it clear that the stronger position is redemptive.

Contemporaries who've come out of the occult are like those "weaker brothers". They cry, "Stay away from all of that! Trust me, it's all occult!" But because they are weaker, they are not yet ready for a redemptive posture. Redemption requires maturity. The redemptive posture being advocated here is for the mature in Christ . . . not the baby Christian and especially not a new Christian coming out of New Age or the occult. Paul's conclusion to the matter is that the stronger must sacrifice for the weaker. It is more important for young, fragile faith to be supported than for the strong to enjoy their freedoms. This is the law of love in all areas. I would not offer Splankna treatment to a new sister in Christ who is fresh from the local coven. I would honor her vulnerability and not let my freedom cause her to stumble.

When it comes to the question of New Age, my ignorance in those early years worked in my favor. I had no idea what the Taoist worldview was. I was uninformed about how Hindus viewed "energy". I was introduced simply to the observation of energy and its behavior as described by quantum physics. I did as we all naturally do. I interpreted that information through my worldview. I saw it automatically through a biblical lens and concluded that it is God's ongoing will that causes the particles to move. I did not have to fight to redeem energy. I was unhindered by the lie. But if I had been a Hindu when I learned about energy, I would have made a different conclusion. I am sure that believers who have come out of Taoism or Hinduism, for instance, would have a much more difficult time taking a redemptive posture toward Energy Psychology. They have much more to fight with—similar to the Christian who has come out of witchcraft. As weaker brothers it might seem impossible to separate observation from false conclusion. In these cases I encourage the strong to relinquish their freedoms and protect the faith of the weak.

While I push for the redemptive posture in all things, I do recognize that the mere fact that all things are redeemable does not mean they're uniform. The issue does not lie in practice, but not all practices are equal. Some things support a walk in the light and some practices make it more difficult. *"Everything is permissible—" but not everything is beneficial* (1 Cor. 10:23). While I can be in heart's trouble in any camp, there are of course still easier areas and more strenuous areas. Yes, I can be in heart's sin during intercession for instance, but it isn't as likely as it would be in some other arenas. Yes, I can redeem energy tools, but it isn't effortless. It takes maturity and vigilance.

"Self-testing" is a good example of this point. Because a muscle will naturally respond to energetic shifts that go off in the body, it is possible to use one's own muscle for testing. There are many styles of self-testing in contemporary use. Theoretically, and in practice, this is no different than muscle testing using another person's arm. However, in Splankna training conferences we do not train people to self-test; we do not endorse it as a practice. If "the issue does not lie in practice", then why do we disavow self-testing? Is it because surrogate testing is safe and self-testing is sinful? No. It is because the issue lies in heart's posture. In self-testing it is much easier to become overly *reliant* on testing. It is far easier to slip into areas of questioning that are not within the domain of one's own heart and body. It is far too easy to fall into heart's dependence on a false source. A person is much more vulnerable through self-testing to end up self-testing every passing thought or question; the heart becomes idolatrous. Simple knowledge of the danger does not stop a fallen heart from falling. I am prone to the same temptation that befell Adam and Eve. Even in Christ it takes close attention to keep the flesh in check. Yes, I can lose command of my heart within any practice and maintain it in any practice, but some are easier than others.

It must be acknowledged that the plea of this book is to the strong. Admittedly it is a rigorous endeavor. But there is a time and place for rigor. While the weaker brother must be taken into account and protected, he also needs to be stretched toward growth. The stronger brothers need to challenge one another as well. Too often we gear all of our teaching to the lowest common denominator in an effort to protect the weak and welcome the seeker. We have adopted a false humility that precludes anyone from being the "stronger".

John Eldredge illustrates this beautifully in his frustration with Christian responses to recent, headlining, pastoral sin. He heard a sermon from another local pastor attempting to be gracious. This pastor said in effect, "Far be it for us to judge. Any one of us could fall prey to the same temptation at any time." John retorts in effect, "Really? Is there no acknowledgement of growth in Christ? Do I remain at ground zero in development all of my life?" Surely we can admit without slipping into arrogance that there is growth in Christ—that there are not only the seekers among us but also the strong. In the name of sensitivity, humility, and loving one another we can lose track of the meat. We can forget to feed and challenge the strong. And in doing so, we can lose our redemptive passion and responsibility. I believe that some of the current frustration with the American model of church is that the Gospel is being dumbed-down beyond recognition. The strong are bored. Yes, there are easier landscapes than these to traverse, but ease has never been our highest goal.

Does anybody know what happened to the steak knives?

CHAPTER 12

# The Impassioned Plea

*"When I stand before God at the end of my life, I would hope*
*that I would not have a single bit of talent left, and could say,*
*'I used everything you gave me'." —Erma Bombeck*

*"Life shouldn't be a journey to the grave with the intention of*
*arriving safely in a pretty and well preserved body,*
*but rather, to skid in broadside, thoroughly used up,*
*totally worn out, and loudly shouting,*
*'Wow! What a ride! Thank You Lord!'" —Beth Moore*

S o after all of this discussion of redemption and boundaries and rigor, why bother? Why work this hard? If it's admittedly more difficult to walk these kinds of lines, why not just stay in the illusory safe zone and manage my heart from there? Why work to bring Energy Psychology back into the Kingdom? Why fight for the redemption of energy or anything else?

First, because *inherently*, without the enemy's twist, everything belongs to God. He called it all "good". Because He has a million beautiful secrets in His creation and a million powerful modes of healing, and this is one of them. It's worth redeeming Energy Psychology because of Emily, who suffered for nine years with debilitating fibromyalgia and has now been pain-free for three years. Because of Jack, whose obsessive-compulsive disorder was so severe, it took him an hour to leave his house in the morning and two hours to get to bed each night but who has nearly forgotten what that was like after five years of freedom. Because of Renee, who was able to overcome years of painful infertility by getting to the root of her fears of mothering and who now enjoys two beautiful blessings from God. Because of Jerrod, who fought with everything he could to deny a deep attraction to other men and now reports that he no longer has the slightest pull. You know a thing by its fruit.

There are many more stories like these. For many years now God has consistently used these tools through myself and through many other Splankna practitioners to heal the hearts of His people and raise up His Body for such a time as this. He can and will do the same with other tools that have been so far too hastily rejected by the Body of Christ.

The fruit of Splankna Therapy is wonderful, but God has limitless ways to bring about our healing. He does not need Splankna. He does not need quantum physics. The redemptive posture matters for larger reasons.

We are redeeming energy because *redemption* matters to God.

We are surrounded by these issues in our culture, and they are not going away. We cannot afford to be ignorant or fearful. We find ourselves strapped into a cultural ship that is careening into darkness faster each day. Professor of Theology Norman Geisler states that the New Age Movement is "the most dangerous enemy of Christianity in the world today . . . more dangerous than secular humanism." It has so permeated Western thought that it is becoming difficult to distinguish its influence anymore. It seems normal. And witchcraft? Wicca is an official, legal religion in the U.S. and a fast-growing one at that. Judges have ruled that witches must be allowed to lead prayers at local government meetings and that Wiccan convicts must be provided with requested "sacred objects" so they can perform spells in their cells. Witches in the armed services have even formed covens and routinely "worship" on U.S. military bases. There are estimates of as many as three million practicing witches in the United States.

How is the Christian to respond? We do not represent God well when our only reaction to this cultural decay is condemnation. Paul did not just explain to the Athenians their sin; he offered them the truth that was already beneath their lie. We have a similar opportunity now. When our response to the New Age prophet or the deceived Wiccan is merely judgment, we may be taking care of ourselves and our own purity, but we do nothing to foster the truth beyond our steeples. Any time we stop at judgment and fear, we discredit our God. He does not stop there. His *"kingdom come"* does not stop there, and we are its ambassadors.

We are at a stage in American sociological history where we have largely rejected the reductionist/materialist model and are pendulum-swinging toward pantheism. The Church has an unprecedented opportunity to provide the voice of truth in the midst of this reactionism. We are the bearers of the Truth that *does* offer a paradigm for authentic holism. The Truth of the Word of God *does* present the mind/body/spirit paradigm. We must offer this answer. We must take the offense.

What if we were wild and crazy and we even went a step further than protecting ourselves with wise boundaries . . . even a step further than redemption . . . all the way to the offense? What if we made it our practice to go to an unbelieving acupuncturist, let's say, and rather than just putting the blood of Jesus between us to protect ourselves, we prayed beforehand that all of their ungodly power would be blocked and that the Holy Spirit would take over? What if we invited the Spirit of God to move through the practitioner and his tools so powerfully that afterward he has to ask me, "What happened?", and I have a chance to introduce him to the Living God?

We think that by huddling together in the "safe zone" of Christian culture, we have done our job. Now we just try to hold it together until we're rescued (and of course always try to bring as many others into the huddle as possible). The world discovers something miraculous in God's creation; all we can do is cover our ears in the name of holiness. We were never intended to live on the defense. The gates of hell shall not prevail against us. It is not only our privilege, but our responsibility to be on the offense in our culture. It is our birthright to forge out into the world and proclaim all things HIS. Science uncovers something new and the enemy jumps on it with his definition and stamp of ownership and we are nowhere to be found. He has no competition. Why do you think he is so quick to claim it? It is not accidental that tools like these are so prospered by his camp. They are powerful. The enemy uses them because they work. They work because God created them to.

I believe it is a great offense to God that as He allowed us to discover the quantum level of His creation, the enemy got to claim it uncontested. New Age has been allowed to write its name all over it so indelibly that we don't even know how to argue anymore. Energy has never belonged to the enemy any more than anything else in God's creation; His claim must not continue to go uncontested.

Up until this point the Church's main concern has been purity; well it should be. But let's take the next step. Let's not leave it at sin management. That was never the point. The point is to announce and advance the Kingdom of God. Yes, we need to be clear about the lies and sin involved in New Age and witchcraft. But clarity is not established for its own sake or even for the sake of purity alone but for *dominion*. Let's not be content with holiness but see it as our foundation for reigning and disseminating the Kingdom in all its forms, including healing. *For everything God created is good, and nothing is to be rejected if it is received with thanksgiving, because it is consecrated by the word of God and prayer* (1 Tim. 4:3-5). Yes, it is difficult to deal with energy tools and maintain the boundaries of Truth. Yes there's work, but there's also life—life worth fighting for and the reputation of our Creator to defend.

I worry sometimes that our generation is in danger of being the man in the parable who buried his talent. Remember the story in Matthew 25? The landlord gives 10 talents to one, five to another, and just one talent to the last servant. When the landlord returned the first two had invested and multiplied what they had, but the third man had buried his. He reasoned that he'd better play it safe. His master is tough. "You are a hard man. You reap where you do not sow." "I may not have accomplished anything, but at least I stayed holy. I didn't mess up." Multiplication takes risk. We're so quick to proclaim the dangers of "excess"—so quick to say, "You've gone too far." But we don't consider the equal and opposite danger in which we are entrenched—never moving at all—living a whole lifetime in the huddle, on the defense, when his gates never could have prevailed against us.

Had we moved.

I would rather make the opposite mistake. I would rather be guilty of going a little too far a time or two because I took the talent He gave me and knocked myself out. It has been the call on my life to redeem the tools of Energy Psychology for the Kingdom of God. But in the end, it doesn't really matter whether or not Christians use any particular healing practice. What matters is living redemptively in such a time as this. What matters is living like we're the ones who win in the end. The *Christians* should have been the ones to teach the world about the power of intention and the spoken word. The *Christians* should have been the first to proclaim God's quantum miracle and His call to partnership. The enemy must not continue to get credit for God's creation. It is our responsibility and honor to take back everything He's tried to claim. He will not easily steal another ounce of the Glory of God. Not on my watch.

May you be restless in the huddle and gutsy outside of it.


May you have eyes to see His light in the darkest places
and the strength to proclaim it.


May you enjoy the expansive reach of our God.

# Appendix

Many other practices are outlined in Scripture that seem like witchcraft even though they are not. Here are a few other examples:

God appeared to Abraham at the oak tree of Moreh in Genesis 12 to tell him that He would give that land to his descendants. (Gen. 12:6-7)

Joseph is mentioned as having a "divining cup." In the times of the Mishna the Jews of the Roman period used wine instead of oil for this purpose.[72]

God used many men to speak His inspired words to His people Israel. He spoke to them directly and symbolically; the same way pagan oracles received their transcriptions. An oracle was a supernatural message that was received, but not from God. "Oracle" is simply the pagan term for what God calls "prophesy" (cf. Jer. 4:10-12; Ezek. 18:9-13). Paul relates a healing oracle/prophesy (2 Cor. 12:9) and prophesies about the last days

(1 Cor. 15:51-52; 1 Thess. 4:16-17a). Others predict suffering (1 Thess. 3:4; Acts 21:11; 11:28; 18:9-10; 23:11; 27:23-24).[73] These inspired predictions were given by the Lord.

Saul resorted to the sin of necromancy (with the witch of Endor) only after the Lord did not answer him, either by dreams, or by Urim, or by prophets (1 Sam. 28:6). This account implies that the other means mentioned were *legitimate* tools, e.g. dreams, Urim, and the prophets.

The name of God, *YHWH*, was never pronounced (Exod. 3:13-15). Jesus has a name inscribed which no one knows but Himself (Rev. 19:12). Early cultures believed that the divine name could invoke blessing and drive away evil. Similarly, baptism in the early church was administered 'in the name' of God and Jesus (Matt. 28:19), and healings were accomplished in Jesus' name (Acts 3:6).

In the plains of Moab, Balak offered a great amount of money to Balaam, a known oracle, to put a curse on the Israelites so that Balak could defeat them (Num. 22). Rather than smiting him for his occult practices of cursing/blessing, God used him instead to bless Israel. Balaam is apparently a diviner turned prophet under divine constraint.

Leviticus explains Israel's ritual ceremony for the cleansing of their sin. The priest over Israel would take a "scapegoat," lay his hands on it, and transfer the sins of Israel onto it. He would then send it out of the city bearing upon it "all their iniquities unto a land not inhabited." The goat was to remove their sin from them in this manner. A later modification was made indicating that they did not consider this symbolic but literal. The priest was not only to take the goat out of the city, he was instructed then to push the beast down a steep mountainside, ensuring its death. The reason of this barbarous custom was that on one occasion the scapegoat returned to Jerusalem after being set free, which was considered such an evil omen that its recurrence was prevented for the future by the death!

# References

1.  Rachel S. Herz, "Aromatherapy Facts and Fictions: A Scientific Analysis of Olfactory Effects on Mood, Physiology and Behavior," in the *International Journal of Neuroscience*, vol. 119, Num. 2 (2009), pp. 263-290.

2.  Victoria E. Slater, "Healing Touch," in *Fundamentals of Complementary and Alternative Medicine*, ed. Marc S. Micozzi (New York: Churchill Livingstone, 1995), pp. 121-36.

3.  C.W. Weber, "Daoism," in *Dictionary of Contemporary Religion in The Western World*, ed. Christopher Partridge (InterVarsity Press: 2002), p. 224.

4.  Douglas R. Groothuis, *Unmasking The New Age*, (Downers Grove, IL: Intervarsity Press, 1986), p. 98.

5.  Fritjov Capra, *The Tao of Physics*, Fontanal Collins, 1976.

6.  Hugh Ross, *The Fingerprint of God* (Orange, CA: Promise Publishing, 1989), p. 134.

7.  Heisenberg, *Physics and Philosophy*, pp. 58, 81.

8.  Pearcey, N., & Thaxton, C. B. (1994). The soul of science: Christian faith and natural philosophy. *Turning point Christian worldview series* (199). Wheaton, Ill.: Crossway Books.

9.  A.C. Ahn, A.P. Colbert, B.J. Anderson, O.G. Martinsen, R. Hammerschlag, S. Cina, P.M. Wayne, H. Langevin. Electrical properties of acupuncture points and meridians: a systematic review. *Bioelectromagnetics*, 29: 245-56, 2008.

10. Burton Goldberg, *Alternative Medicine: The Definitive Guide*, (Berkeley, CA, 2002), p. 62.

11. Darras, Jean Claude, Albarede, P., and de Vernejoul, Pierre. "Nuclear Medicine Investigation of Transmission of Acupuncture Information." *Acupuncture in medicine, Journal of the British Medical Acupuncture Society*, March 31, 1993, pp. 22-28.

12. Cho, Z. H. "New Finding of the Correlation Between Acupoints and Corresponding Brain Cortices Using Functional MRI." *Proceedings of National Academy of Sciences* 95 (1998): pp. 2670-2673.

13. David Feinstein, Ph.D., "Energy Psychology In Disaster Relief." *Traumatology.* vol 14:1 (2008), pp. 124-137.

14. James P. Carter, "If EDTA Chelation Therapy Is So Good, Why Is It Not More Widely Accepted?" *Journal Of Advancement In Medicine*, vol. 2 ½ (1989), pp. 213-226.

15. Candace Pert, Ph.D., *Molecules of Emotion*, (NY: Simon & Schuster, 1997).

16. Jay Haley and Chloe Madanes, *Strategic Family Therapy*, (Jossey-Bass, 1981).

17. James R. Lane, "The Neurochemistry of Counter-Conditioning: Acupressure Desensitization in Psychotherapy." *Energy Psychology: Theory, Research and Treatment*, vol. 1 (2009), p. 1.

18. David Feinstein, Ph.D., Donna Eden and Gary Craig, *The Promise of Energy Psychology*, (New York, NY: The Penguin Group, 2005).

19. J. H. Diepold & D. Goldstein, "Thought Field Therapy and QEEG changes in the treatment of trauma: A case study." *Traumatology*, vol. 15 (2008), pp. 85-93.

20. Gary Craig, *Emotional Freedom Technique*, (Santa Rosa, CA: Energy Psychology Press, 2008).

21. Website, www.NetMindBody.com

22. Francine Shapiro, Ph.D., *Eye Movement Desensitization and Reprocessing; Basic Principles, Protocols and Procedures*, (New York, NY: Guilford Press, 2001).

23. Carolyn Wadsworth, Ruth Krishnan, Mary Sear, Jean Harrold and David Neilsen, "Intrarater Reliability of Manual Muscle Testing and Hand-held Dynametric Muscle Testing." *Journal of the American Physical Therapy Association*, vol. 67 num. 9 (1987), pp. 1342-1347.

24. Dr. Douglas Groothuis, *Unmasking the New Age* (InterVarsity Press, 1986), p. 18.

25. J. Keel, *The Eighth Tower*. New York: Signet, 1975, preface.

26. D. Berkson, *The Foot Book: Healing the Body Through Reflexology*, (New York: Barnes & Noble Books, 1977), p. 8.

27. B. Walker, Hindu World, London 1968, keyword: Kundalini.

28. Dr. Douglas Groothuis, *Unmasking the New Age* (InterVarsity Press, 1986), p. 30.

29. Wood, D. R. W., & Marshall, I. H. (1996). *New Bible Dictionary (3rd ed.)* (289). Leicester, England; Downers Grove, Ill.: InterVarsity Press.

30. Barbour, *Issues in Science and Religion*, p. 119.

31. W.E. Vine, Merrill F. Unger, *Vine's Expository Dictionary of Biblical Words*, (Thomas Nelson Publishers, 1995).

32. David Wilcox, *Nightshift Watchman*, and *Turning Point*, (1987).

33. Dr. Neil T. Anderson and Dr. Michael Jacobson, *The Biblical Guide To Alternative Medicine* (Ventura, CA: Regal, 2003), p. 93.

34. Winfred Corduan, *Neighboring Faiths* (InterVarsity Press, 1998), pp. 189-310.

35. George Orwell, *A Collection Of Essays* (Harvest Books, 1970).

36. Neale Donald Walsch, *Conversations with God*, (Hampton Roads, 1997), p. 6.

37. Zuck, R. B., Bock, D. L., & Dallas Theological Seminary (1996, c1994). *A biblical theology of the New Testament* (189). Chicago: Moody Press.

38. Aristotle, Book 12 (Greek " ") of his *Metaphysics*

39. Leslie Lyall, Ph.D., Confucianism, in: Anderson N. (ed), The world's religions, London 1975, pp. 219-27.

40. Douglas R. Groothuis, *Unmasking The New Age*, (Downers Grove, IL: Intervarsity Press, 1986), p. 106.

41. Werner Gitt, *In The Beginning Was Information*, (Christliche Literatur – Verbreitung, December 2000).

42. Walter Brueggemann, *Isreal's Praise*, (Augsburg Fortress Publishers, March 1988).

43. Monte Kline, Ph.D., "New Age Paranoia," *Christian Health Counselor*, March/April 1988, 1-2.

44. Douglas R. Groothuis, *Unmasking The New Age*, (Downers Grove, IL: Intervarsity Press, 1986), p. 107.

45. Dr. Neil T. Anderson and Dr. Michael Jacobson, *The Biblical Guide To Alternative Medicine* (Ventura, CA: Regal, 2003), p. 190-191.

46. Translation from the Greek by Ludwig Edelstein. From *The Hippocratic Oath: Text, Translation, and Interpretation*, by Ludwig Edelstein. Baltimore: Johns Hopkins Press, 1943.

47. Elliot Miller, (2009) *The Christian, Energetic Medicine, 'New Age Paranoia,'* Retrieved August 20, 2009, from The Christian Research Institute, Web site: http://www.equip.org/articles/the-christian-energetic-medicine-new-age-paranoia-

48. Achtemeier, P. J., Harper & Row, P., & Society of Biblical Literature. (1985). *Harper's Bible Dictionary* (1st ed.) (1137). San Francisco: Harper & Row.

49. Achtemeier, P. J., Harper & Row, P., & Society of Biblical Literature. (1985). *Harper's Bible Dictionary* (1st ed.) (594). San Francisco: Harper & Row.

50. Louw, J. P., & Nida, E. A. (1996, c1989). *Greek-English lexicon of the New Testament: Based on semantic domains* (electronic ed. of the 2nd edition.) (1:544). New York: United Bible Societies.

51. Dr. Neil T. Anderson and Dr. Michael Jacobson, *The Biblical Guide To Alternative Medicine* (Ventura, CA: Regal, 2003), p. 95.

52. Achtemeier, P. J., Harper & Row, P., & Society of Biblical Literature. (1985). *Harper's Bible Dictionary* (1st ed.) (594). San Francisco: Harper & Row.

53. Geisler, N. L. (1999). *Baker Encyclopedia of Christian Apologetics*. Baker Reference Library (476–477). Grand Rapids, Mich.: Baker Books.

54. Girdlestone, R. B. (1998). *Synonyms of the Old Testament: Their bearing on Christian doctrine*. (297). Oak Harbor, WA: Logos Research Systems, Inc.

55. Achtemeier, P. J., Harper & Row, P., & Society of Biblical Literature. (1985). *Harper's Bible Dictionary* (1st ed.) (595). San Francisco: Harper & Row.

56. Achtemeier, P. J., Harper & Row, P., & Society of Biblical Literature. (1985). *Harper's Bible Dictionary* (1st ed.) (595). San Francisco: Harper & Row.

57. Wood, D. R. W., & Marshall, I. H. (1996). *New Bible Dictionary* (3rd ed.) (279–280). Leicester, England; Downers Grove, Ill.: InterVarsity Press.

58. Achtemeier, P. J., Harper & Row, P., & Society of Biblical Literature. (1985). *Harper's Bible Dictionary* (1st ed.) (595). San Francisco: Harper & Row.

59. Walvoord, John F., Roy B. Zuck, and Dallas Theological Seminary. *The Bible Knowledge Commentary: An Exposition of the Scriptures*. Wheaton, IL: Victor Books, 1983-c1985.

60. Janet Ferrar and Stewart Ferrar, *A Witches Bible Compleat* (New York, NY: Magickal Childe Publishing Inc., 1981), p. 175.

61. Geisler, N. L. (1999). *Baker Encyclopedia of Christian Apologetics*. Baker Reference Library (477). Grand Rapids, Mich.: Baker Books.

62. Geisler, N. L. (1999). *Baker Encyclopedia of Christian Apologetics*. Baker Reference Library (478). Grand Rapids, Mich.: Baker Books.

63. Wood, D. R. W., & Marshall, I. H. (1996). *New Bible Dictionary* (3rd ed.) (713). Leicester, England; Downers Grove, Ill.: InterVarsity Press.

64. Achtemeier, P. J., Harper & Row, P., & Society of Biblical Literature. (1985). *Harper's Bible Dictionary* (1st ed.) (1108). San Francisco: Harper & Row.

65. Achtemeier, P. J., Harper & Row, P., & Society of Biblical Literature. (1985). *Harper's Bible Dictionary* (1st ed.) (28). San Francisco: Harper & Row.

66. Wood, D. R. W., & Marshall, I. H. (1996). *New Bible Dictionary* (3rd ed.) (714–715). Leicester, England; Downers Grove, Ill.: InterVarsity Press.

67. Achtemeier, P. J., Harper & Row, P., & Society of Biblical Literature. (1985). *Harper's Bible Dictionary* (1st ed.) (578). San Francisco: Harper & Row.

68. Wiersbe, W. W. (1996, c1989). *The Bible Exposition Commentary* (1 Jn 3:4). Wheaton, Ill.: Victor Books.

69. *The Holy Bible: New International Version.* 1996, c1984 (electronic ed.) (Nu 21:8-9). Grand Rapids: Zondervan.

70. Diane Stein, *Essential Reiki* (Freedom, Calif.: Crossing Press, 1995).

71. Agnes Sanford, *The Healing Light* (Ballantine Books, revised 1983).

72. Negev, A. (1996, c1990). *The Archaeological encyclopedia of the Holy Land* (3rd ed.). New York: Prentice Hall Press.

73. Achtemeier, P. J., Harper & Row, P., & Society of Biblical Literature. (1985). *Harper's Bible Dictionary* (1st ed.) (732). San Francisco: Harper & Row.

# Index

9-G sequence 61

Acupuncture 12, 39, 40, 41, 53, 56, 168, 169

Agreement(s) 67, 71, 153, 156, 157, 158, 159

Alarm point 45

Algorithms 25, 56, 57, 160

Allopathic 33, 34, 48

Apostle Paul 170

Aromatherapy 34

Bilateral stimulation 60, 61, 159, 160

Breath 35, 75, 88, 97, 98, 99, 105, 110, 143

Buddhism 70, 92

Callahan, Roger 25, 56-61, 155, 159

Chakra 75, 115

Chay 99

Chiropractic 25, 29, 41, 56, 58

Co-reigner 104

Craig, Gary 57

Crystal ball 162

Divination 29, 122, 125, 126, 127, 128, 129, 141, 162

Divinity 74, 75, 76, 78, 79, 80, 92, 93, 102, 111, 113, 116, 122, 123, 133

Effect 35, 53, 55, 57, 58, 104, 127, 141, 147, 168, 173

Emotion 34, 44, 45, 52, 53, 56, 58, 59, 69, 100, 104, 105, 106, 152, 153, 154, 155, 158, 162

Emotion Chart 152, 153, 154

Emotional Freedom Technique 57

Energy 11, 12, 27, 28, 29, 31, 33, 34, 35, 36, 39, 40, 41, 43, 44, 46, 51, 52, 54, 55, 56, 58, 59, 60, 61, 62, 63, 64, 66, 67, 71, 72, 75, 84, 97, 98, 99, 100, 101, 102, 103, 105, 106, 108, 109, 112, 113, 114, 115, 116, 117, 121, 122, 123, 142, 145, 149, 152, 153, 160, 161, 164, 166, 167, 168, 169, 171, 172, 175, 176, 178, 179

Energy Psychology 11, 12, 28, 29, 31, 33, 39, 41, 43, 44, 46, 51, 52, 54, 55, 56, 59, 60, 61, 62, 63, 64, 66, 99, 100, 103, 108, 112, 114, 116, 122, 145, 149, 153, 160, 161, 168, 172, 175, 176, 179

Evil 66, 73, 74, 78, 82, 92, 97, 98, 108, 118, 122, 129, 133, 137, 138, 139, 140, 141, 142, 143, 144, 145, 182

Eye Movement Desensitization and Reprocessing (E.M.D.R.) 55, 59, 60, 61

Forgiveness 10, 69, 154, 155

Groothuis, Douglas 70

Heisenberg's Uncertainty Principle 36

Hierarchy 86, 87, 89, 110, 132, 168

Hinduism 70, 92, 109, 172

Holistic 44, 81, 113, 163

Idolatry 125, 129, 137, 141, 168, 170

Intention 37, 38, 51, 52, 53, 54, 56, 58, 59, 61, 64, 78, 80, 100, 102, 103, 104, 105, 114, 129, 140, 142, 145, 147, 153, 154, 161, 164, 167, 168, 169, 171, 175, 179

Invocation/invoke 141, 147, 165, 168, 182

Circuitry + Intention 51, 52, 53, 54, 58, 61, 64, 105, 153, 154, 161, 167

Kundalini Serpent 75

Logos 100, 101, 102, 103, 105, 167

Lordship 12, 85, 87, 140, 141, 144, 148, 165, 168

Magic 122, 123

Meridians 39, 40, 43, 58, 152

Monism 70, 74, 85, 86, 89, 110

Muscle Testing 29, 62, 63, 81, 82, 142, 161, 162, 163, 172

Neshamah 97, 98

Neuro-Emotional Technique (N.E.T.) 29, 55, 58, 152

New Age 12, 25, 27, 31, 37, 60, 61, 64, 65, 66, 67, 69, 70, 71, 72, 73, 74, 75, 77, 78, 79, 80, 81, 82, 83, 85, 87, 88, 89, 91, 92, 93, 94, 95, 97, 99, 103, 105, 106, 107, 108, 109, 110, 111, 112, 113, 114, 119, 122, 130, 132, 133, 149, 161, 164, 166, 168, 171, 176, 177, 178

Newtonian Physics 37, 167

Observation/Conclusion 36, 37, 38, 59, 80, 90, 92, 104, 106, 112, 113, 114, 115, 116, 118, 140, 171, 172

Occult 116, 121, 122, 130, 171, 182

Ouija Board 27, 29, 162

Pantheism 70, 72, 74, 85, 110, 118, 177

Particles 35, 36, 37, 38, 39, 41, 84, 103, 104, 105, 106, 110, 113, 167, 171

Personhood 67, 71, 85, 102, 110, 132, 147, 168

Pharisees 30, 135, 140

Phobia 26, 46, 53, 54, 56, 158

Pneuma 99

Prana 34

Prayer 30, 64, 144, 147, 151, 152, 158, 163, 165, 166, 169, 178

Protocol Chart 152, 160

Qi 35

Quantum 11, 12, 35, 36, 37, 38, 39, 41, 43, 52, 64, 84, 100, 103, 104, 105, 106, 113, 114, 166, 167, 171, 176, 178, 179

Quantum physics 11, 12, 35, 38, 84, 103, 105, 106, 113, 167, 171, 176

Rebellion 129, 137, 141, 145, 168, 170

Redemption 11, 87, 119, 131, 133, 135, 137, 139, 141, 143, 145, 147, 171, 175, 176, 177

Redemptive 29, 107, 109, 111, 113, 115, 117, 119, 138, 142, 144, 161, 163,

165, 167, 169, 170, 171, 172, 173, 176

Reiki 164, 165, 166, 167

Ruwach 97, 98, 99

Satanism 122

Self-testing 172, 173

Set 11, 24, 65, 76, 89, 94, 103, 111, 122, 153, 154, 155, 159, 182

Shapiro, Francine 59

Special knowledge 82, 124, 125, 128, 129, 147, 162, 163, 168

Special power 124, 125, 127, 128, 141, 146, 162, 168

Spirit Guide 164, 165, 170

Splankna 9, 11, 12, 13, 29, 51, 55, 58, 61, 63, 64, 149, 150, 152, 153, 155, 156, 157, 158, 159, 160, 161, 162, 163, 171, 172, 176

Subatomic 36, 70, 84

Subconscious 44, 45, 50, 51, 60, 62, 63, 80, 81, 84, 114, 115, 150, 151, 157, 163, 166

Tapping sequence 26, 56

The Secret 76, 77, 78, 124, 136

Theory/theories of change 24, 34, 46, 47, 48, 49, 51, 52, 66, 69

Third party 162, 165, 168

Thought Field Therapy 25, 26, 29, 55, 56, 57, 59

Touch 16, 52, 55, 58, 59, 60, 90, 143, 145, 154, 164, 166, 167, 168

Trauma 45, 46, 52, 53, 54, 56, 57, 59, 60, 61, 62, 64, 93, 143, 152, 153, 154, 155, 156, 157, 158, 159, 160, 162, 163

Trauma Emotion 162

Triple Warmer 57, 61

Truth 12, 30, 38, 68, 71, 73, 75, 76, 77, 86, 94, 106, 107, 109, 110, 111, 113, 115, 118, 130, 140, 169, 177, 179

Universal consciousness 166

Universalism 70, 91

Walker, Scott 58, 152

White witchcraft 128, 129

Witch 122, 126, 132, 133, 147, 182

Witchcraft 12, 25, 64, 119, 121, 122, 123, 124, 125, 127, 128, 129, 130, 131, 132, 133, 134, 135, 137, 138, 139, 140, 141, 142, 143, 144, 145, 146, 147, 149, 161, 162, 163, 164, 167, 168, 172, 176, 178, 181

Yoga 80, 109, 144

The Splankna Therapy Institute provides training for Licensed Christian Counselors, Ministers, Lay Counselors, and other Christian practitioners such as Chiropractors, Massage Therapists, etc. It is our mission to provide a Christian protocol for Energy Psychology that is accessible to all of the body of Christ. Level 1 Trainings are open to all. There is an Advanced Training open to those who have been through Level 1, and a special Clinical Advanced Training open only to Licensed Mental Health Professionals. At Clinical Advanced we address DSM disorders such as Dissociative Identity Disorder and Schizophrenia. All training conferences are 3 days in length, 9:00am – 5:00pm.

The Splankna Therapy Institute is located in Denver and has annual Level 1 Training Conferences there and in Dallas, Nashville, and Los Angeles as well. So far Advanced Training Conferences are only held in Denver but we expect to expand in the future.

For more information on training, visit our website at *www.splankna.com*, or contact:

Heather Hughes
Heather@Splankna.com
720-210-7077
Splankna Therapy Institute
2121 S. Oneida St., Suite 450
Denver, CO 80224

There are currently over 150 trained Splankna Practitioners around the country. To locate a Practitioner in your area contact:

Tandy Cowles
Tandy@Splankna.com
719-660-7052
Splankna Therapy Institute
2121 S. Oneida St., Suite 450
Denver, CO 80224

Made in the USA
Lexington, KY
02 December 2012